Fodor's InFocus

ARUBA

12
TOP EXPERIENCES

Aruba offers terrific experiences that should be on every traveler's list. Here are Fodor's top picks for a memorable trip.

1 High-Rise Resorts

On a beautiful stretch of Palm Beach, Aruba vacationers can choose among many of the Caribbean's most lavish resorts, with deluxe spas, water-sports centers, fine restaurants, casinos, shops, and nightclubs. *(Ch. 5)*

2 Eagle Beach

Prepare to be dazzled (seriously, bring your sunglasses) by the bright white sand of Eagle Beach, which stretches far and wide on the south-western coast. The beach is popular but rarely overcrowded. *(Ch. 3)*

3 Casinos

Aruba casinos are the real deal, with slots, table games, and sports books for plenty of action. Theaters, restaurants, bars, and cigar shops round out the entertainment. *(Ch. 7)*

4 Horseback Riding

An exciting, romantic way to explore Aruba is on horseback. Take a leisurely beach ride or survey the countryside on trails flanked by cacti, divi-divi trees, and aloe vera plants. *(Ch. 8)*

5 Barhopping Buses

Why drive to a bar when a groovy bus can pick you up at your hotel? Enjoy the journey and the destination as you're shuttled to the liveliest nightspots aboard Aruba's unique party buses. *(Ch. 6)*

6 The Bonbini Festival

Every week this festival at Fort Zoutman showcases steel pan bands and local performing artists. It's both a brisk introduction to Aruba's lively culture and a great place to meet friendly locals. *(Ch. 6)*

7 Scuba Diving

Advanced and novice divers appreciate the plentiful marine life in Aruba's clear waters. Some of the best sites are right offshore, and there are fascinating shipwrecks in both deep and shallow waters. *(Ch. 8)*

8 Sailing

Day sails to remote snorkeling spots, sunset voyages on a catamaran, and champagne-and-dinner cruises are some of the most memorable ways you can spend a day or night in Aruba. *(Ch. 8)*

9 Dining on the Beach

Open-air dining on the beach is a special island experience available at a number of Aruba restaurants. The most romantic tables are at Passions on the Beach and Flying Fishbone. *(Ch. 4)*

10 Snorkeling

Thanks to water visibility of 90 feet and closed-in sites such as Barcadera Reef, snorkelers can view many of the same underwater spectacles as divers. Huge sea fans, nurse sharks, and hawksbill turtles are common sights. *(Ch. 8)*

11 Arikok National Park

At Aruba's sprawling national park you can explore caves, play on sand dunes, or hike Mt. Yamanota, the island's highest peak. History you can see includes Arawak petroglyphs and remnants of Dutch settlements. *(Chs. 2, 8)*

12 Oranjestad

Aruba's capital is a delight to explore on foot. Pastel-painted buildings of typical Dutch design face its palm-lined central thoroughfare, and there are numerous boutiques and shops. *(Chs. 2, 9)*

CONTENTS

DID YOU KNOW?

Aruba's waters are exceptionally clear, especially on the leeward side of the island, where underwater visibility can be up to 90 feet.

ABOUT THIS GUIDE

Fodor's Recommendations
Everything in this guide is worth doing—we don't cover what isn't—but exceptional sights, hotels, and restaurants are recognized with additional accolades. Fodor's Choice★ indicates our top recommendations. Care to nominate a new place? Visit Fodors.com/contact-us.

Trip Costs
We list prices wherever possible to help you budget well. Hotel and restaurant price categories from $ to $$$$ are noted alongside each recommendation. For hotels, we include the lowest cost of a standard double room in high season. For restaurants, we cite the average price of a main course at dinner or, if dinner isn't served, at lunch. For attractions, we always list adult admission fees; discounts are usually available for children, students, and senior citizens.

Hotels
Our local writers vet every hotel to recommend the best overnights in each price category, from budget to expensive. Unless otherwise specified, you can expect private bath, phone, and TV in your room. For expanded hotel reviews, facilities, and deals visit Fodors.com.

Restaurants
Unless we state otherwise, restaurants are open for lunch and dinner daily. We mention dress code only when there's a specific requirement and reservations only when they're essential or not accepted. To make restaurant reservations, visit Fodors.com.

Credit Cards
The hotels and restaurants in this guide typically accept credit cards. If not, we'll say so.

Top Picks
★ Fodor's Choice

Listings
⊠ Address
⊠ Branch address
✆ Mailing address
☎ Telephone
🖷 Fax
⊕ Website
✉ E-mail

☜ Admission fee
⊙ Open/closed times
Ⓜ Subway
✛ Directions or Map coordinates

Hotels & Restaurants
🏨 Hotel
🛏 Number of rooms
🍴 Meal plans

✗ Restaurant
🍸 Reservations
🏛 Dress code
☰ No credit cards
$ Price

Other
⇨ See also
☞ Take note
🏌 Golf facilities

EXPERIENCE
ARUBA

1

WHAT'S WHERE

1 Palm Beach. Aruba's largest high-rise hotels are along Palm Beach, which is one of the island's best swimming beaches thanks to the calm waters. You'll have your choice of big resorts, restaurants, casinos, and water sports here. It's always action packed and a great place to people-watch.

2 Eagle Beach. Aruba's "low-rise" hotel area is lined with smaller boutique resorts and time-share resorts. Eagle Beach is wider than Palm Beach, so it's not as crowded and is the island's best big beach.

3 Manchebo Beach. Just south of Eagle Beach, Manchebo has rougher surf, is rarely crowded, and has one of the broadest expanses of sand. The beach here merges into Druif Beach, a lovely stretch that is dominated by the sprawling Divi resort complex.

4 Oranjestad. Aruba's capital is a great place to go for shopping, restaurants, and nightlife or to make arrangements for a tour or other activity. Although the city has no beachfront and few hotels, the beautiful Renaissance Aruba made its own beach overlooking the sea and has a private island with adult-only and family-friendly beaches for guests.

California Pt.

Arashi Beach

Boca Catalina Beach

Malmok Beach

Malmok Reef

Fisherman's Hut

Tierra del Sol Golf Course

Mt. Altovista

1 Palm Beach

Noord

Tanki Leendert

Paradera

2 Eagle Beach

Manchebo Beach

3

Druif Beach

Druif Bay

Cruise Ship Terminal

4 Oranjestad

Surfside Beach

Reina Beatrix International Airport

1 A/B
2 A/B
6 A/B
4 A/B
7 A/B
1 A/B

J.E. Irausquin Blvd.

KEY
Beaches

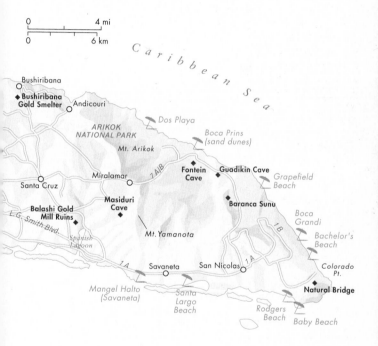

C a r i b b e a n   S e a

0   4 mi
0   6 km

Bushiribana
◆ Bushiribana
Gold Smelter
Andicouri

ARIKOK
NATIONAL PARK
Dos Playa
Boca Prins
(sand dunes)
Mt. Arikok

Miralamar
Santa Cruz

7 A/B

Fontein
Cave
Guadikin Cave
Grapefield
Beach

Masiduri
Cave
◆
Baranca Sunu
◆

Balashi Gold
Mill Ruins
◆

L.G. Smith Blvd.

Spanish
Lagoon

Mt. Yamanota

Boca
Grandi

Bachelor's
Beach

1 B

Colorado
Pt.

1 A

Savaneta
San Nicolas

1 A

Natural Bridge
◆

Mangel Halto
(Savaneta)
Santa
Largo
Beach

Rodgers
Beach
Baby Beach

PLANNER

Island Activities

Since soft, sandy **beaches** and turquoise waters are the biggest draws in Aruba, they can be crowded. Eagle Beach is the best the island has to offer.

Aruba also comes alive by night, and has become a true **party hot spot**. The **casinos**—not as elaborate as those in Las Vegas—are among the best of any Caribbean island.

Restaurants can be pricey, but many are very good.

Diving is good in Aruba, though perhaps not as great as in Bonaire.

Near-constant breezes and tranquil, protected waters have proven to be a boon for **windsurfers,** who have discovered that conditions on the southwestern coast are ideal for their sport.

A largely undeveloped region in Arikok National Wildlife Park is the destination of choice for visitors wishing to **hike** and explore some wild terrain.

Logistics

Getting to Aruba: Aruba is 2½ hours from Miami and 4½ hours from New York. Smaller airlines connect the Dutch islands in the Caribbean, often using Aruba as a hub. Travelers to the United States clear Customs and Immigration before leaving Aruba.

Nonstops: There are nonstop flights from Atlanta (Delta), Boston (American, JetBlue, US Airways), Charlotte (US Airways), Chicago (United—weekly), Fort Lauderdale (Spirit—weekly), Houston (Continental—weekly), Miami (American), Newark (Continental), New York–JFK (American, Delta, JetBlue), New York–LGA (Continental—weekly), Philadelphia (US Airways—twice weekly), and Washington, D.C.–Dulles (United), though not all flights are daily.

On the Ground

A taxi from the airport to most hotels takes about 20 minutes. It costs about $22 to hotels along Eagle Beach, $25 to the high-rise hotels on Palm Beach, and $18 to hotels downtown. Buses are a good option for traveling around the island and are especially convenient for shorter trips; they run only once an hour, but the price is right (a two-trip card for $4 or a day pass for $10 that buys you an unlimited number of rides).

Renting a Car: Rent a car to explore independently, but for just getting to and around town, taxis are preferable, and you can use tour companies to arrange your activities. Rent a four-wheel-drive vehicle if you plan to explore the island's natural sights.

Dining and Lodging on Aruba

Aruba is known for its large, luxurious high-rise resorts and vast array of time-shares. But the island also has a nice selection of smaller, low-rise resorts for travelers who don't want to feel lost in a large, impersonal hotel complex. If you're on a budget, consider booking one of the island's many apartment-style units, so you can eat in sometimes instead of having to rely on restaurants exclusively.

Since the all-inclusive resort scheme hasn't taken over Aruba, as it has many other islands, you'll find a wide range of good independent and resort-based restaurant choices. There's a variety of restaurants in Oranjestad, the island's capital, but you'll also find good choices in the resort areas of Eagle and Palm beaches, as well as Savaneta and San Nicolas.

Hotel and Restaurant Costs

Prices in the restaurant reviews are the average cost of a main course at dinner or, if dinner isn't served, at lunch; taxes and service charges are generally included.

Prices in the hotel reviews are the lowest cost of a standard double room in high season, excluding taxes, service charges, and meal plans (except at all-inclusives).

Prices for rentals are the lowest per-night cost for a one-bedroom unit in high season.

Tips for Travelers

Currency: You probably won't need to change any money if you're coming from the United States. American currency is accepted almost everywhere in Aruba, though you might get some change back in local currency—the Aruban florin, also called the guilder.

Electricity: Aruba's current is 110 volts, just as in the United States.

Nightlife: Aruba is renowned for its nightlife and casinos; the legal drinking and gambling age is 18.

Traffic: Oranjestad traffic can be heavy during rush hour. Allow a bit of extra time if you're trying to get into town for dinner.

Water: You can safely drink the water in Aruba. It's one of the few places in the world to rely almost completely on desalinated seawater for drinking.

WHEN TO GO

Aruba's high season runs early December–mid-April. During this season you're guaranteed the most entertainment at resorts and the most people with whom to enjoy it. It's also the most fashionable and most expensive time to visit, both for people staying a week or more and for cruise-ship passengers coming ashore. During this period hotels are solidly booked, and you must make reservations at least two or three months in advance for the very best places (and to get the best airfares). During the rest of the year hotel prices can drop 20%–40% after April 15.

Climate

Aruba doesn't really have a rainy season and rarely sees a hurricane—one reason why the island is more popular than most during the off-season (mid-May–mid-November), when the risk of Atlantic hurricanes is at its highest. Temperatures are constant (along with the trade winds) year-round. Expect daytime temperatures in the 80s Fahrenheit and nighttime temperatures in the high 70s year-round.

Festivals and Events

January–March: Carnival. Weeks of parties and cultural events precede this two-day street party in late February or early March.

May: Aruba Soul Beach Music Festival. This concert features international artists and takes place over two days on Memorial Day weekend at a different resort every year. ⊕ *www.soulbeach.net*

July: Aruba Hi-Winds. This windsurfing and kiteboarding event takes place over six days, usually in late June or early July. It brings windsurfers of all skill levels from more than 30 different countries to compete off the beaches at Fisherman's Huts at Hadikurari and is considered by some to be the best in the Caribbean. ⊕ *www.hiwindsaruba.com*

August: Aruba Regatta. Three days of racing and parties, this is one of Aruba's annual highlights. ⊕ *www.aruba-regatta.com*

September: Caribbean Sea Jazz. A two-day musical extravaganza features international and local jazz and pop performers. ⊕ *www.caribbeanseajazz.com*

November: Aruba International Beach Tennis Tournament. The largest beach tennis competition in the Caribbean attracts competitors from all over the globe to a big party on Eagle Beach.

Year-Round: Bon Bini Festival. Every Tuesday evening Fort Zoutman comes alive with music and local folk dancing.

GREAT ITINERARIES

Are you perplexed about which of Aruba's many beaches is best or how to spend your time during one of the island's rare rainy days? Below are some suggestions to guide you. There are also a few ideas on how to create a night that completes a perfect day.

A Perfect Rainy Day

Even though Aruba is outside the hurricane belt, you may find yourself with the rare rainy day, or you might just want a break from the tropical heat if you overdid the sunbathing. That's a perfect time to explore some of the museums and the art gallery in downtown Oranjestad and ride the free eco-trolley around the newly refreshed Main Street and see what's on offer. You can head to modern, multilevel Palm Beach Plaza for all kinds of shopping, entertainment, and movies. They also have a food court and several lunch options in the immediate vicinity. You can also enjoy some first-rate pampering at one of the island's many premium spas. Or how about a couple's massage by the sea? If you want more action, the casinos are always ready to receive you. Some are open 24 hours a day, and sometimes they offer daytime bingo as well, for something different to do.

A Perfect Day at the Beach

If you didn't bring your own, borrow or rent snorkel gear at your hotel so that you can fully appreciate the calm water and all its inhabitants. Eagle Beach is the island's best, and you can grab a space under one of the many palapa umbrellas if you arrive early enough. The water here is fine for both swimming and snorkeling. As the sun goes down, hop back across the road to the very casual Pata Pata Bar at La Cabana Resort for happy hour. There's no need to change.

A Perfect Night of Romance

One Of Aruba's most romantic experiences is a sunset cruise. Try a voyage on the 43-foot sailing yacht *Tranquilo,* which includes drinks. For dinner, Pinchos Grill & Bar is hard to beat, even on an island filled with romantic dining options. End the evening with a walk—hand in hand—along the waterfront.

ARUBA WITH KIDS

Aruba has a kid-loving culture, and its slogan "One Happy Island" extends to young visitors as well. The island is a reasonably short flight away from most of the Eastern Seaboard (about three to six hours), and there are familiar sights such as fast-food places that help make kids feel more comfortable. Though the island may not offer all of the distractions of a theme park holiday, it has more than enough to keep most kids occupied during a family vacation.

Where to Stay

Virtually all the best places for families to stay are on or along the beaches that run the length of the western side of the island. The island's east coast is rocky with rough seas and offers little in the way of accommodations. Aruba is a sun-and-sand destination, so most families will find their dollar best spent picking a hotel as close to the beach as their budget will allow. An ocean view isn't a necessity, but ease of access to one of the beaches is recommended.

Best High-Rise Resorts. Choose a high-rise resort if you want a great variety of amenities and activities. Most of Aruba's high-rise resorts offer kids' programs and are generally found along **Palm Beach**. The large **Westin Aruba** right on the beach has a terrific kids' program that includes a "director of fun"

and a program called Love Your Family. The **Hyatt Regency Aruba Beach Resort** offers an extensive kids' program and has many family-fun activities such as horseback riding, various water sports, and tennis. The **Ritz-Carlton Aruba** has the Ritz Kidz program with seriously creative activities inspired by Jean-Michel Cousteau's (Jacques Cousteau's son) and his Ocean Futures Society.

Best Low-Rise Resorts. Aruba's smaller low-rise properties don't offer as many amenities as the high-rises, but they provide a relaxing, laid-back vibe, and some do have kids' programs. Low-rise properties are mostly found along **Eagle Beach, Manchebo Beach, and Druif Beach** and are often less crowded. **Amsterdam Manor** on Eagle Beach is a good value-hotel with kitchenettes and a mini–grocery store on site so families can save money and enjoy a relaxing stay. At **Divi Aruba All-Inclusive** on Druif Beach, children under 18 stay free when accompanied by two adults, and their kids' camp even offers Papiamento language lessons. The beach here is gorgeous, and all nonmotorized water sports are included in the price.

Beaches

Palm Beach is wide and offers powdery white sand, generally calm waters, and plenty of nearby amenities like food and beverages. Families that want a bit more room to move around away from the crowds might find **Druif** and **Manchebo** beaches more to their liking, but there aren't as many options for chair rentals and refreshments. Sprawling **Eagle Beach** offers the best of all worlds with fewer crowds and a range of amenities within easy walking distance.

Water Activities

Snorkeling, swimming, kayaking, and sailing are some of the things that keep families coming back to Aruba year after year. Most hotels and condos offer inexpensive equipment rentals for a day in the water. Seasoned junior snorkelers will find the viewing pretty dull off the major beaches, so organized tours such as those offered by **De Palm Tours** and **Red Sail Sports**, which explore more remote coves, may provide more of a satisfying underwater experience. **De Palm Island** offers a variety of water activities for kids, including snorkeling and a water park that makes for a great day in the sun.

Though a bit pricey for larger families, the **Atlantis Submarine Tour** will likely entertain even the most jaded teen.

Land Activities

The **Aruba Ostrich Farm** is an interesting short excursion that can entertain young children, but Philip's Animal Garden is where they will be entertained for hours by its many fun creatures and a huge playground. The **Butterfly Farm** is also a lovely experience for all ages, and if you go early in your holiday, you can return for free as many times as you want with your original admission voucher. The **Donkey Sanctuary Aruba** is also a must-visit. The friendly residents there love to have visitors. (Bring apples and carrots!) And for evening activities, **Paseo Herencia** has a gorgeous waltzing waters show three times a night in their amphitheater/courtyard and a cool old-fashioned carousel. They also often have cultural shows and bouncy castles for kids, and there are movie cinemas there as well. **Palm Beach Plaza Mall** right behind it also has glow-in-the-dark bowling, movies, a huge modern video arcade, and a food court for a fun night out off the beach.

Families looking more adventure and encounters with local wildlife can try a day of hiking at **Arikok National Park.** Eddy Croes of **Aruba Nature Sensitive Tours** is a former ranger at the park and will turn the excursion into a fun learning experience.

DID YOU KNOW?

On January 1, 1986, Aruba became an independent entity within the Kingdom of the Netherlands, which consists of the Netherlands, the Netherlands Antilles, and Aruba.

EXPLORING

BALMY SUNSHINE, SILKY SAND, aquamarine waters, natural scenic wonders, outstanding dining, decent shopping, and an array of nightly entertainment . . . Aruba's got it in spades. It's also unusual in its range of choices, from world-class oceanfront resorts equipped with gourmet restaurants and high-dollar casinos to intimate neighborhood motels and diners not far off the beach.

Aruba's wildly sculpted landscape is replete with rocky deserts, cactus clusters, secluded coves, blue vistas, and the trademark divi-divi tree. To preserve the environment while encouraging visitors to explore, the government has implemented an ongoing ecotourism plan. Initiatives include finding ways to make efficient use of the limited land resources and protecting the natural and cultural resources in such preserves as Arikok National Park and the Coastal Protection Zone (along the island's north and east coasts).

Oranjestad, Aruba's capital, is good for shopping by day and dining by night, but the "real Aruba"—with its untamed beauty—is discovered in the countryside. Rent a car, take a sightseeing tour, or hire a cab by the hour to explore. Though remote, the northern and eastern shores are striking and well worth a visit. A drive out past the California Lighthouse or to Seroe Colorado will give you a feel for the backcountry.

The main highways are well paved, but the windward side of the island has some roads that are a mixture of compacted dirt and stones. A car is fine, but a four-wheel-drive vehicle will enable you to better navigate the unpaved interior. Remember that few beaches outside the hotel strip along Palm and Eagle beaches to the west have refreshment stands, so pack your own food and drinks. Aside from those in the infrequent restaurant, there are no public bathrooms outside of Oranjestad.

Traffic is sparse, but signs leading to sights are often small and hand-lettered (this is slowly changing as the government puts up official road signs), so watch closely. Route 1A travels southbound along the western coast, and 1B is simply northbound along the same road. If you lose your way, just follow the bend of the divi-divi trees. They always point toward the resorts.

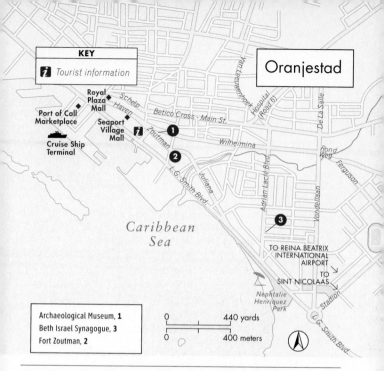

ORANJESTAD AND ENVIRONS

Aruba's capital is easily explored on foot. Its palm-lined central thoroughfare runs between old and new pastel-painted buildings of typical Dutch design (Spanish influence is also evident in some of the architecture). There are a lot of malls with boutiques and shops—the Renaissance mall carries high-end luxury items and designer fashions. A massive renovation in downtown has given Main Street (aka Caya G. F. Betico Croes) behind the Renaissance Resort a whole new lease on life: boutique malls, shops, and restaurants have opened next to well-loved family-run businesses. The pedestrian-only walkway and resting areas have unclogged the street, and the new eco-trolley is free and a great way to get around. At this writing, Linear Park was well and will showcase local merchants and artists. There will be activities along a boardwalk that will eventually run all the way to the end of Palm Beach, making it the longest of its kind in the Caribbean.

TIMING

There's rarely a day when there aren't at least two cruise ships docked in Oranjestad, so the downtown shopping

DID YOU KNOW?

Aruba's first Dutch colonial governor was Peter Stuyvesant, who was also the last Dutch director-general of New Amsterdam, better known today as New York.

festivals. Visitors are always welcome, although it's best to make an appointment to see the synagogue when there's not a service. ⊠ *Adrian Laclé Blvd. 2* ☎ *297/582–3272* ☞ *Free (except high holy days).*

Ft. Zoutman. One of the island's oldest edifices, Aruba's historic fort was built in 1796 and played an important role in skirmishes between British and Curaçao troops in 1803. The Willem III Tower, named for the Dutch monarch of that time, was added in 1868 to serve as a lighthouse. Over time the fort has been a government office building, a police station, and a prison; now its historical museum displays Aruban artifacts in an 18th-century house. This is also the site of the weekly Tuesday night welcome party called the Bon Bini festival with local music, food, and dance. ⊠ *Zoutmanstraat* ☎ *297/582–5199* ☞ *$5* ⊙ *Weekdays 8:30–4.*

MANCHEBO AND DRUIF BEACHES

One beach seamlessly merges with another, resulting in a miles-long stretch of powdery sand peppered with a few low-rise resorts. This part of the island is much less crowded than Palm Beach and great for a morning or evening stroll.

EAGLE BEACH

This area is often referred to as Aruba's low-rise hotel area. It's lined with smaller boutique resorts and time-share resorts. Eagle Beach is considered one of the best beaches in the Caribbean. The white sand here seems to stretch on forever. The water is great for swimming, and there are numerous refreshment spots. Although the beach can get busy during the day, there's never a problem finding a spot, but if you're looking for shade, it's best to stick near one of the hotel bar huts along the beach.

PALM BEACH AND NOORD

The district of Noord is home to the strip of high-rise hotels and casinos that line Palm Beach. The hotels and restaurants, ranging from haute cuisine to fast food, are densely packed into a few miles running along the beachfront. When other areas of Aruba are shutting down for the night, this area is guaranteed to still be buzzing with

Papiamento Primer

CLOSE UP

Papiamento is a hybrid language born out of the colorful past of Aruba, Bonaire, and Curaçao. The language's use is generally thought to have started in the 17th century, when Sephardic Jews migrated with their African slaves from Brazil to Curaçao. The slaves spoke a pidgin Portuguese, which may have been blended with pure Portuguese, some Dutch (the colonial power in charge of the island), and Arawakan. Proximity to the mainland meant that Spanish and English words were also incorporated.

Papiamento is roughly translated as "the way of speaking." (Sometimes the suffix -mentu is spelled in the Spanish and Portuguese way [-mento], creating the variant spelling.) It began as an oral tradition, handed down through the generations and spoken by all social classes on the islands. There's no uniform spelling or grammar from island to island, or even from one neighborhood to another. However, it is beginning to receive some official recognition. A noteworthy measure of the increased government respect for the language is that anyone applying for citizenship must be fluent in both Papiamento and Dutch.

Arubans enjoy it when visitors use their language, so don't be shy. You can buy a Papiamento dictionary to build your vocabulary, but here are a few pleasantries to get you started:

Bon dia. Good morning.

Bon tardi. Good afternoon.

Bon nochi. Good evening/night.

Bon bini. Welcome.

Ajo. Bye.

Te aworo. See you later.

Pasa un bon dia. Have a good day.

Danki. Thank you.

Na bo ordo. You're welcome.

Con ta bai? How are you?

Mi ta bon. I am fine.

Ban goza! Let's enjoy!

Pabien! Congratulations!

Quanto costa esaki? How much is this?

Hopi bon. Very good.

Ami. Me.

Abo. You.

Nos dos. The two of us.

Mi dushi. My sweetheart.

Ku tur mi amor. With all my love.

Un braza. A hug.

Un sunchi. A kiss.

Mi stima Aruba. I love Aruba.

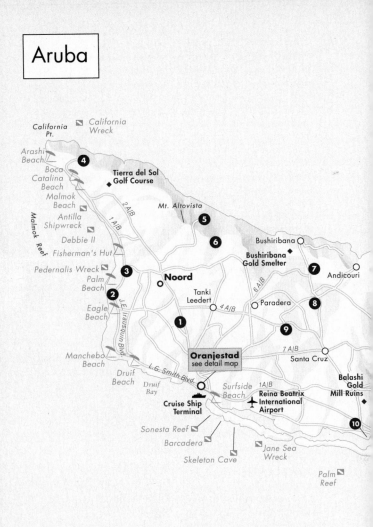

Aruba

California Pt.
California Wreck
Arashi Beach
Boca Catalina Beach
Malmok Beach
Antilla Shipwreck
Debbie II
Fisherman's Hut
Pedernalis Wreck
Palm Beach
Eagle Beach
Manchebo Beach
Druif Beach
Druif Bay
Malmok Reef
J.E. Irausquin Blvd.
L.G. Smith Blvd.

4
Tierra del Sol Golf Course
Mt. Altovista
2 A/B
1 A/B
5
6
Bushiribana
Bushiribana Gold Smelter
7
Andicouri
6 A/B
3
Noord
Tanki Leedert
4 A/B
Paradera
8
1
9
2
7 A/B
Santa Cruz
Balashi Gold Mill Ruins
Oranjestad
see detail map
Surfside Beach
1 A/B
Reina Beatrix International Airport
10
Cruise Ship Terminal
Sonesta Reef
Barcadera
Skeleton Cave
Jane Sea Wreck
Palm Reef

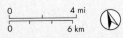

0   4 mi
0   6 km

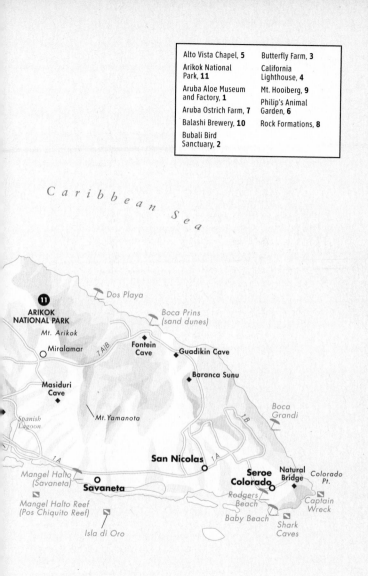

Alto Vista Chapel, **5**	Butterfly Farm, **3**
Arikok National Park, **11**	California Lighthouse, **4**
Aruba Aloe Museum and Factory, **1**	Mt. Hooiberg, **9**
Aruba Ostrich Farm, **7**	Philip's Animal Garden, **6**
Balashi Brewery, **10**	Rock Formations, **8**
Bubali Bird Sanctuary, **2**	

C a r i b b e a n   S e a

11
ARIKOK NATIONAL PARK
Mt. Arikok
○ Miralamar

Dos Playa

Boca Prins (sand dunes)

7 A/B

Fontein Cave

◆ **Guadikin Cave**

◆ **Baranca Sunu**

Boca Grandi

1 B

◆ **Masiduri Cave**

Spanish Lagoon

Mt. Yamanota

1 A

San Nicolas ○

1 A

Seroe Colorado ○

Natural Bridge ◆

Colorado Pt.

Mangel Halto (Savaneta)

Savaneta ○

Rodgers Beach

Captain Wreck

Mangel Halto Reef (Pos Chiquito Reef)

Baby Beach

Shark Caves

Isla di Oro

KEY	
⚲	*Beaches*
◹	*Dive Sites*

Oranjestad Renaissance

Aruba's historic port capital city Oranjestad has always had a colorful Dutch colonial charm, but the past few years has seen a major face-lift and renewal throughout downtown to better accommodate a growing local population and better welcome the million-plus visitors it sees each year. To make the cruise terminal more inviting and the first impression of the city more alluring, all cargo traffic operations have been moved to Barcadera. Some back streets have been closed to traffic, making new pedestrian malls and courtyards that allow visitors to wander past the harbor village and back into the original Main Street (G. F. Betico Croes) area that is two streets behind the harbor. A new free eco-trolley system

makes it easy to explore all corners of the newly refreshed downtown, starting at the cruise terminal and looping throughout the shops, attractions, museums, dining spots, and malls, and reaching right to the public bus terminal. Visitors can hop on and off at will; it travels very slowly so you can get a good look at what's on offer. The recent Oranjestad renaissance has been well received, bringing new businesses and attractions and kicking off a good start to the continuing construction of a new Linear Park that will connect downtown to the main tourist beaches by boardwalk and when completed will become the longest park of its kind in the Caribbean.

activity. Here you can also find the beautiful **St. Ann's Church,** known for its ornate 19th-century altar. In this area Aruban-style homes are scattered amid clusters of cacti.

TOP ATTRACTIONS

★ Fodor's Choice **Butterfly Farm.** Hundreds of butterflies and moths
FAMILY from around the world flutter about this spectacular garden. Guided tours (included in the price of admission) provide an entertaining look into the life cycle of these insects, from egg to caterpillar to chrysalis to butterfly or moth. After your initial visit, you can return as often as you like for free during your vacation. ■ TIP→ Go early in the morning when the butterflies are most active; wear bright colors if you want them to land on you. Early morning is also when you are most likely to see the caterpillars emerge from their cocoons and transform into butterflies or moths

A GOOD TOUR: WESTERN ARUBA

Western Aruba is where you'll likely spend most of your time. All the resorts and time-shares are along this coast, most of them clustered on the oceanfront strip at the luscious Palm and Eagle beaches, in the city of Oranjestad, or in the district of Noord. All the casinos, major shopping malls, and most restaurants are found in this region, as is the airport.

Rent a car and head out on Route 1A toward **Oranjestad** for some sightseeing and shopping. Pick up Route 1B out of town. At a large roundabout turn right and drive for about 1 km (½ mile), then make another right at the first intersection and drive for ½ km (¼ mile) until you reach the fields and factory of **Aruba Aloe**. Head back to the roundabout and pick up Route 4A. Follow this road a short way to the **Ayo and Casibari Rock Formations**. Continue on 4A and follow the signs for **Hooiberg**; if you're so inclined, climb the steps of Haystack Hill. Return on 4B

to 6A and drive a couple of miles to the Bushiribana Gold Smelter. Beyond it on the windward coast is the **Aruba Ostrich Farm**.

From here, take 6B to the intersection of Route 3B, which you'll follow into the town of **Noord**, a good place to stop for lunch. Then take Route 2B, following the signs for the branch road leading to the **Alto Vista Chapel**. Return to town and pick up 2B and then 1B to reach the **California Lighthouse**. In this area you can also see Arashi Beach (a popular snorkeling site) and the Tierra del Sol golf course. From the lighthouse, follow 1A back toward Palm Beach. On the way, stop at the **Butterfly Farm** and the **Bubali Bird Sanctuary**.

TIMING

If you head out right after breakfast, you can just about complete the above tour in one very full day. If you want to linger in Oranjestad's shops or go snorkeling along the beach, consider breaking the tour up into two days.

as well. ✉ *J. E. Irausquin Blvd., Palm Beach* ☎ *297/586–3656* ⊕ *www.thebutterflyfarm.com* 🎫 *$15* ⊗ *Mon.–Sun. 8:30–4:30 (last tour at 4).*

★ Fodor's Choice **Philip's Animal Garden.** This nonprofit exotic
FAMILY animal rescue and rehabilitation foundation is a wonderful, child-friendly attraction. Each guest is given a bag of treats for the animal residents, which include monkeys, peacocks, an emu, an ocelot, an alpaca, and many other types of

Alto Vista Chapel, on the windy northwest coast of Aruba, was built in 1750.

creatures you're not likely to see on Aruba. There's a large playground and ranch so little ones can run. It is also a stop on some tours. ⊠ *Alto Vista 116, Noord* ☎ *297/593–5363* ⊕ *www.philipsanimalgarden.com.*

WORTH NOTING

Bubali Bird Sanctuary. More than 80 species of migratory birds nest in this man-made wetland area inland from the island's strip of high-rise hotels. Herons, egrets, cormorants, coots, gulls, skimmers, terns, and ducks are among the winged wonders in and around the two interconnected artificial lakes that make up the sanctuary. Perch up on the wooden observation tower for great photo ops. ⊠ *J. E. Irausquin Blvd., Noord* ☎ *Free.*

WESTERN TIP (CALIFORNIA DUNES)

No trip to Aruba is complete without a visit to the California Lighthouse, and it's also worth exploring the rugged area of the island's Western tip. This is the transition point between Aruba's calmer and rougher coasts. Malmok Beach and Arashi Beach are popular for windsurfing and excellent for grabbing dramatic sunset photos.

TOP ATTRACTIONS

California Lighthouse. Declared a national monument in 2014, the landmark lighthouse on the island's eastern tip is being restored to its original glory. It was named after a merchant ship that sunk nearby called the *Californian,* a tragedy that spawned its construction. Built in 1910, it has been a famous Aruba attraction for decades and a typical stop on most island tours. ⊠ *Arashi, Noord.*

WORTH NOTING

Alto Vista Chapel. Meaning "high view," Alto Vista was built in 1750 as the island's first Roman Catholic Church. The simple yellow and orange structure stands out in bright contrast to its stark desertlike surroundings, and its elevated location affords a wonderful panoramic view of the northwest coast. Restored in 1953, it's still in operation today with regular services and also serves as the culmination point of the annual walk of the cross at Easter. You will see small signposts guiding the faithful to the Stations of the Cross all along the winding road to its entrance. This landmark is a typical stop on most island tours. ⊠ *Alto Vista Rd.* ✛ *Follow the rough, winding dirt road that loops around the island's northern tip, or from the hotel strip, take Palm Beach Road through 3 intersections and watch for the asphalt road to the left just past the Alto Vista Rum Shop.*

SANTA CRUZ

Though not a tourist hot spot (by Aruba standards) this town in the center of the island offers a good taste of how the locals live. It's not architecturally interesting, but there are some intriguing little restaurants and snack shacks. Local shops offer something a bit different from the usual tourist fare, and the prices are reasonable.

WORTH NOTING

Mt. Hooiberg. Named for its shape (*hooiberg* means "haystack" in Dutch), this 541-foot peak lies inland just past the airport. If you have the energy, you can climb the 562 steps to the top for an impressive view of Oranjestad (and Venezuela on clear days).

Aruba's divi-divi trees are always bent toward the west, where you'll find the best beaches.

SAVANETA

The Dutch settled here after retaking the island in 1816, and it served as Aruba's first capital. Today it's a bustling fishing village with a 150-year-old *cas di torto* (mud hut), the oldest dwelling still standing on the island.

SAN NICOLAS

During its oil-refinery heyday, Aruba's oldest village was a bustling port and the island's economic hub. As demand for the oil dwindled and tourism rose, attention shifted to Oranjestad and the island's best beaches. These past few years, San Nicolas has been enjoying a renaissance: every Thursday night there's Caribbean Festival, a minicarnival in the streets. There's also a new ballpark, a carnival village, and a museum and workshop. A perennial draw is the legendary Charlie's Bar & Restaurant, a family-run business that's been around for over 70 years. It's packed with paraphernalia left behind by generations of visitors. Aruba's legal red-light district is also here; much like Amsterdam's red-light district, it's quiet, regulated, and controlled.

SEROE COLORADO

This surreal ghost town was originally built as a community for American oil workers who came to run the Lago Refinery in the 1950s. There were 700 residents, an English-language school, a social club, a beach club, a hospital, a local newspaper, and a bowling alley. Today, organ-pipe cacti form the backdrop for the sedate white-washed cottages. Most people visit for the **natural bridge**. Keep bearing east past the community, continuing uphill until you run out of road. You can then hike down to the cathedral-like formation. It's not too strenuous, but take care as you descend. Be sure to follow the white arrows painted on the rocks, as there are no other directional signs. The raw elemental power of the sea, which created this fascinating rock formation, complete with hissing blowholes, is stunning.

ARIKOK NATIONAL PARK AND ENVIRONS

Nearly 20% of Aruba has been designated part of Arikok National Park, which sprawls across the eastern interior and the northeast coast. The new, eco-friendly visitor center is built entirely of sustainable South American hardwood, uses solar panels for clean energy, and cools the building with an underground water basin. The park is the keystone of the government's long-term ecotourism plan to preserve Aruba's resources and showcases the island's flora and fauna. Other highlights include ancient Arawak petroglyphs, ruins of a gold-mining operation at Miralmar, and remnants of Dutch peasant settlements in Masiduri. Within the confines of the park are Mt. Arikok and the 620-foot Mt. Yamanota, Aruba's highest peak. The natural pool (*conchi*) is a popular snorkeling destination and a beautiful natural phenomenon.

Anyone looking for geological exotica should head for the park's caves, found on the northeastern coast. The ancient drawings of Fontein Cave were made by indigenous peoples many centuries ago (rangers are on hand to offer explanations). Bats are known to make appearances—don't worry, they won't bother you. Although you don't need a flashlight because the paths are well lighted, it's best to wear sneakers.

A GOOD TOUR: EASTERN ARUBA

Take Route 1A to Route 4B and visit the Balashi Gold Smelter ruins and **Frenchman's Pass**. Return to 1A and continue your drive past Mangel Halto Beach to **Savaneta**, a fishing village and one of several residential areas that have examples of typical Aruban homes. Follow 1A to **San Nicolas**, where you can meander along the main promenade, pick up a few souvenirs, and grab a bite to eat. Heading out of town, continue on 1A until you hit a fork in the road; follow the signs toward **Seroe Colorado**, with the nearby natural bridge and the Colorado Point Lighthouse. From here, follow the signs toward Rodgers' Beach, just one of several area shores where you can kick back for a while. Nearby Baby Beach, with calm waters and beautiful white sand, is a favorite spot for snorkelers.

To the north, on Route 7B, is Boca Grandi, a great windsurfing spot. Next is Grapefield Beach, a stretch of white sand that glistens against a backdrop of cliffs and boulder formations. Shortly beyond it, on 7B, you'll come into **Arikok National Park**, where you can explore caves and tunnels, play on sand dunes, and tackle Mt. Yamanota, Aruba's highest elevation. Farther along 7B is **Santa Cruz**, where a wooden cross stands atop a hill to mark the spot where Christianity was introduced to the islanders. The same highway will bring you all the way into Oranjestad.

TIMING

You can see most of eastern Aruba's sights in a half day, though it's easy to fill a full day if you spend time relaxing on a sandy beach or exploring the trails in Arikok National Park.

TOP ATTRACTIONS

Arikok National Park. Covering almost 20% of the island's landmass, this protected preserve of arid, cacti-studded outback has interesting nature and wildflife. Start at the modern Visitor Centre to get information on native animals and see short films about what to look out for in the park. Then take a guided tour with a park ranger to unearth hidden secrets. Hiking maps for all levels of hikers are free, and in-depth maps of the park and its attractions are also available for download online at their website. Some trails lead to glorious seaside coastal views and you can also traverse the park by car (roads are rough, four-wheel drive is recommended), but a guided tour will help you understand the significance of the region and help

2

Cunucu Houses

Pastel houses surrounded by cacti fences adorn Aruba's flat, rugged *cunucu* ("country" in Papiamento). The features of these traditional houses were developed in response to the environment. Early settlers discovered that slanting roofs allowed the heat to rise and that small windows helped to keep in the cool air. Among the earliest building materials was *caliche*, a durable calcium-carbonate substance found in the island's southeastern hills. Many houses were also built using interlocking coral rocks that didn't require mortar (this technique is no longer used, thanks to cement and concrete). Contemporary design combines some of the basic principles of the earlier homes with touches of modernization: windows, though still narrow, have been elongated; roofs are constructed of bright tiles; pretty patios have been added; and doorways and balconies present an ornamental face to the world beyond.

you find attractions like the caves on the northeastern coast. Baranca Sunu, the so-called Tunnel of Love, has a heart-shape entrance and naturally sculpted rocks farther inside. Fontein Cave, which was used by indigenous peoples centuries ago, is marked with ancient drawings. Bats make their home in the caves—don't worry, they won't bother you, but it's best to wear sneakers, because ground bugs can be bothersome. No one is allowed in the park after sundown, but they do offer full-moon guided hikes. There are no facilities past the visitor center, so bring plenty of water and sunscreen and wear good shoes if you are on foot, the terrain is very rocky. ⊠ *San Fuego 70* ☎ *297/585–1234* ⊕ *www.arubanationalpark.org* ☎ *$11* ☉ *Daily 8–4 (ticket sales end at 3:30).*

Aruba Ostrich Farm. Everything you ever wanted to know about the world's largest living birds can be found at this farm. A large *palapa* (palm-thatched roof) houses a gift shop and restaurant that draws large bus tours, and tours of the farm are available every half hour. This operation is virtually identical to the facility in Curaçao; it's owned by the same company. ⊠ *Makividiri Rd., Paradera* ☎ *297/585–9630* ⊕ *www.arubaostrichfarm.com* ☎ *$12* ☉ *Daily 9–4.*

Rock Formations. The massive boulders at Ayo and Casibari are a mystery, as they don't match the island's geological makeup. You can climb to the top for fine views of the arid

countryside. The main path to Casibari has steps and hand-rails, and you must move through tunnels and along narrow steps and ledges to reach the top. At Ayo you can find ancient pictographs in a small cave (the entrance has iron bars to protect the drawings from vandalism). At the base there is a new café/bar/restaurant open for lunch, and their dinner at night when lit up with colored lights around the rocks is surreal. Some party-bus tours stop there for dinner at the end of their journey. ✉ *Paradera* ✛ *Access to the rock formations at Casibari is via Tanki Hwy. 4A; you can reach Ayo via Rte. 6A. Watch carefully for the turnoff signs near the center of the island on the way to the windward side.*

BEACHES

THE BEACHES ON ARUBA ARE LEGENDARY: the solid seven miles of beachfront along its west coast are baby-powder-soft, blindingly white sand carpets that smile over vast expanses of clear azure water with varying degrees of surf action. The waters of Palm Beach in front of the high-rise resort strip are typically pond-still placid, whereas the waves on the low-rise resort strip on Eagle Beach are typically restless and rolling. The beaches on the northeastern side are unsafe for swimming because of strong currents and rough swells, but they are worth seeking out for their natural beauty and romantic vistas. Swimming on the sunrise side of the island is best done in San Nicolas at Baby Beach, named for its calm, toddler-friendly waters.

Arashi Beach. This is the local favorite, a ½-mile (1-km) stretch of gleaming white sand with a rolling surf and good snorkeling. It can get busy on weekends, especially Sunday with local families bringing their own picnics, but during the week it is typically quiet, though Tierra del Sol Resort now provides transportation to it for their guests. **Amenities:** some shade palapas. **Best for:** swimming; walking. ⊠ *West of Malmok Beach, on west end.*

FAMILY **Baby Beach.** On the island's eastern tip (near the now-closed refinery), this semicircular beach borders a placid bay of turquoise water that's just about as shallow as a wading pool—perfect for families with little ones. A small coral reef basin at the sea's edge offers superb snorkeling, but do not pass the barrier as the current is extremely strong outside of the rocks. The new JADS dive shop offers snorkel and dive rentals, and their full-service bar and restaurant also offers a shower and washrooms and a small children's playground. **Amenities:** food and drink; clamshell shade rentals. **Best for:** snorkeling; swimming; walking. ⊠ *Near Seroe Colorado, on east end.*

Boca Catalina. A fairly isolated strip off a residential area, this tiny white-sand cove attracts snorkelers with its shallow water filled with fish. Swimmers will also appreciate the calm conditions. There aren't any facilities nearby, however, so pack provisions and your own snorkel gear. It's popular with locals on weekends. **Amenities:** none. **Best for:** snorkeling; swimming. ⊠ *Between Arashi Beach and Malmok Beach, north of intersection of Rtes. 1B and 2B.*

Boca Grandi. This is *the* choice for the island's best kiteboarders and expert windsurfers, even more so than Fisherman's Huts. But the currents are strong so it's not safe for casual

Baby Beach is a great spot for the family.

swimming. It's very picturesque, though, and a perfect spot for a picnic. It's a few minutes from San Nicolas; look for the big red anchor or the kites in the air. **Amenities:** none. **Best for:** kiteboarding; walking; windsurfing. ✉ *Near Seagrape Grove, on east end, San Nicolas.*

Boca Prins. You'll need a four-wheel-drive vehicle to make the trek to this strip of coastline, which is famous for its backdrop of stunning sand dunes. Near the Fontein Cave and Blue Lagoon, the beach itself is small, but with two rocky cliffs and crashing waves, it's as romantic as Aruba gets. The water is rough, and swimming is prohibited. It's a perfect picnic stop. There's also a small snack bar with burgers, sandwiches, and smoothies. Wear sturdy shoes, as the entrance is rocky. **Amenities:** food and drink; toilets. **Best for:** surfing; walking. ✉ *Off Rte. 7A/B, near Fontein Cave.*

Dos Playa. One of the most photogenic picnic spots on the island, this beach is two coves divided by limestone cliffs. One is treasured by surfers for its rolling waves; the other looks placid but has a current that is far too strong for swimming—you have to settle for sunbathing only. The best access is by four-wheel drive, as it's within the boundaries of rugged Arikok National Park. **Amenities:** none. **Best for:** solitude; surfing; walking. ✉ *Arikok National Park, just north of Boca Prins.*

The Divi-Divi Tree

Like a statuesque dancer in a graceful flat-back pose, the *watapana*, or divi-divi tree, is one of Aruba's hallmarks. Oddly enough, this tropical shrub is a member of the legume family. Its astringent pods contain high levels of tannin, which is leached out for tanning leather. The pods also yield a black dye. The tree has a moderate rate of growth and a high drought tolerance. Typically it reaches no more than 25 feet in height, with a flattened crown and irregular, forked branches. Its leaves are dull green, and its inconspicuous yet fragrant flowers are pale yellow or white and grow in small clusters. Thanks to constant trade winds, the divi-divis serve as a natural compass: they're bent toward the island's leeward—or western—side, where most of the hotels are.

Druif Beach. Fine white sand and calm water make this beach a fine choice for sunbathing and swimming. It's the base beach for the Divi collections of all-inclusive resorts so amenities are reserved for guests. Locals like it, too, and often camp out here as well with their own chairs and coolers. The beach is accessible by bus, rental car, or taxi, and it's walking distance to stores. **Amenities:** parking. **Best for:** sunbathing; swimming. ⊠ *Parallel to J. E. Irausquin Blvd., near Divi resorts, south of Punta Brabo.*

★ **Fodor'sChoice** **Eagle Beach.** Aruba's most photographed beach and widest by far, especially in front of the Manchebo resort, Eagle Beach is not only a favorite with visitors and locals, but also of sea turtles. More sea turtles nest here than anywhere else on the island. This pristine stretch of blinding white sand and aqua surf frequently ranks ranks among the best beaches in the world. Many of the hotels have facilities on or near the beach, and refreshments are never far away, but chairs and shade palapas are reserved for guests only. **Amenities:** food and drink; toilets. **Best for:** sunset; swimming; walking. ⊠ *J. E. Irausquin Blvd., north of Manchebo Beach.*

Fisherman's Huts (*Hadicurari*). Beside the new Ritz-Carlton, Fisherman's Huts is a windsurfer's and kiteboarder's haven. Swimmers might have a hard time avoiding all the boards going by, as this is the nexus of where lessons take place for both sports, and it's always awash in students and experts and board hobbyists. It's a gorgeous spot to just sit and watch the sails on the sea. Only drinks and small snacks are available at the operator's shacks. No washrooms, but the Ritz lobby is nearby in a pinch. **Amenities:** food. **Best for:** kiteboarding; windsurfing. ⊠ *North of Aruba Marriott Resort, Palm Beach.*

Malmok Beach (*Boca Catalina*). On the northwestern shore, this small, nondescript beach borders shallow waters that stretch 300 yards from shore. There are no snack or refreshment stands here, but shade is available under the thatched umbrellas. It's the perfect place to learn to windsurf. Right off the coast here is a favorite haunt for divers and snorkelers—the wreck of the German ship *Antilla*, scuttled in 1940. **Amenities:** none. **Best for:** solitude; snorkeling. ⊠ *At end of J. E. Irausquin Blvd., Malmokweg.*

Manchebo Beach (*Punta Brabo*). Impressively wide, the white, sandy shoreline in front of the Manchebo Beach Resort is where officials turn a blind eye to the occasional topless sunbather. This beach merges with Druif Beach, and most locals use the name Manchebo to refer to both. **Amenities:** food and drink; toilets. **Best for:** swimming. ⊠ *J. E. Irausquin Blvd. at Manchebo Beach Resort.*

Mangel Halto (*Savaneta*). With a sunken wreck near the coast and a lot to see outside the bay, this is one of the most popular spots for shore diving, but be aware that currents are strong once you're outside the cove. It's also popular for picnics, and a wooden dock and stairs into the ocean make getting into the water easy. It's not often crowded, as most people head straight under the waves. **Amenities:** toilets. **Best for:** snorkeling; swimming. ⊠ *Between Savaneta and Pos Chiquito, San Nicolas.*

Palm Beach. This is the island's most populous and popular beach running along the high-rise resorts and it's crammed with every kind of water-sports activity and food-and-drink emporium imaginable. It's always crowded no matter the season, but it's a great place for people-watching, sunbathing, swimming, and partying, and there are always activities happening such as the increasingly popular beach tennis. The water is pond-calm and the sand is powder-fine. **Amenities:** food and drink; shade; toilets; water sports. **Best for:** partying; people-watching; sunbathing; swimming; water sports. ⊠ *J. E. Irausquin Blvd. between Westin Aruba Resort and Marriott's Aruba Ocean Club.*

FAMILY **Rodger's Beach.** Near Baby Beach on the island's eastern tip, this beautiful curving stretch of sand is only slightly marred by its proximity to the tanks and towers of the now defunct oil refinery at the bay's far side. Swimming conditions are excellent here. The snack bar at the water's edge has beach-equipment rentals and a shop. Drive around the refinery perimeter to get here. **Amenities:** food and drink; water sports. **Best for:** swimming. ⊠ *Next to Baby Beach, on east end, San Nicolas.*

4

WHERE TO EAT

THERE ARE A FEW HUNDRED RESTAURANTS on Aruba, from elegant eateries to seafront shacks, so you're bound to find something to tantalize your taste buds. You can sample a wide range of cuisines—Italian, French, Argentine, Asian, and Cuban, to name a few—reflecting Aruba's extensive blend of cultures. Chefs have to be creative on this tiny island because of the limited number of locally grown ingredients: *maripampoen* (a vegetable that's often stewed with meat and potatoes), *hierba di hole* (a sweet-spicy herb used in fish soup), and *shimarucu* (a fruit similar to the cherry) are among the few. Hot sauce made from local Madame Janette peppers is on every table, and the seafood du jour is always a good choice.

Although most resorts offer better-than-average dining, don't be afraid to try one of the many excellent independent places. Ask locals about their favorite spots; some of the lesser-known restaurants offer food that's reasonably priced and definitely worth sampling.

Most restaurants on the western side of the island are along Palm Beach or in downtown Oranjestad, both easily accessible by taxi or bus. If you're heading to a restaurant in Oranjestad for dinner, leave about 15 minutes earlier than you think you should; in-town traffic can get ugly once beach hours are over. Some restaurants in Savaneta (Flying Fishbone) and San Nicolas (Charlie's Restaurant & Bar) are worth the trip; a car is the best way to get there. Breakfast lovers are in luck. For quantity, check out the buffets at the Hyatt, Marriott, or Westin Aruba Resort, Spa & Casino resorts, or local joints such as DeliFrance.

ARUBA DINING PLANNER

ISLAND SAMPLER

Aruba Gastronomic Association: Dine-Around Program *(AGA)*. To give visitors an affordable way to sample the island's eclectic cuisine, the Aruba Gastronomic Association has created a Dine-Around program involving more than 30 island restaurants. Savings abound with all kinds of different packages. Other programs, such as gift certificates and coupons for dinners at the association's VIP member restaurants are also available. You can buy Dine-Around tickets using the association's online order form, through travel agents, or at the De Palm Tours sales desk in many hotels. Participating restaurants and conditions change frequently; the AGA website has the latest information.

Best Bets for Aruba Dining

With the many restaurants to choose from, how will you decide where to eat? Fodor's writers and editors have selected their favorite restaurants in the Best Bets lists below. Fodor's Choice properties represent the "best of the best." Find specific details about a restaurant in the full reviews.

Fodor's Choice: Amuse Bistro; Barefoot; Charlie's Restaurant & Bar; Cuba's Cookin'; Elements; Flying Fishbone; L.G. Smith's Steak & Chop House, Madame

Janette, Pinchos Grill & Bar; Quinta del Carmen.

Best Budget Eats: Arubaville; Casibari Cafe.

Best for Families: Waka Waka Safari Restaurant.

Most Romantic: The Old Man & The Sea; Passions on the Beach; Ruinas del Mar; Screaming Eagle.

Best for Local Aruban Cuisine: Gasparito Restaurant & Art Gallery; Old Cunucu House; Papiamento.

4

✉ *Rooi Santo 21, Noord* ☎*297/586–1266, 914/595–4788 in the U.S.* ⊕*www.arubadining.com.*

PRICES AND DRESS

Aruba's elegant restaurants—where you might have to dress up a little (jackets for men, sundresses for women)—can be pricey. If you want to spend fewer florins, opt for the more casual spots, where being comfortable is the only dress requirement. A sweater draped over your shoulders will go a long way against the chill of air-conditioning. If you plan to eat in the open air, bring along insect repellent in case the mosquitoes get unruly.

RESERVATIONS

To ensure that you get to eat at the restaurants of your choice, make some calls or visit the website when you get to the island—especially during high season—to secure reservations. Note that on Sunday you may have a hard time finding a restaurant that's open for lunch, and that many eateries are closed for dinner Sunday or Monday.

TIPPING

Most restaurants add a service charge of 15%. It's not necessary to tip once a service charge has been added to the bill, but if the service is exceptional, an additional tip of 10% is always appreciated. If no service charge is included on the final bill, then leave the customary tip of 15%–20%.

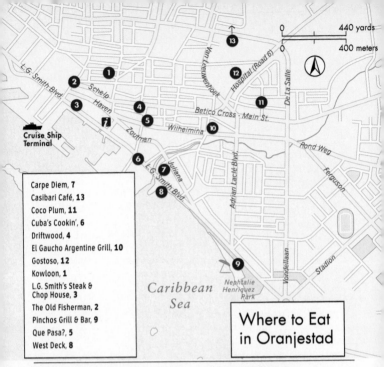

Carpe Diem, **7**

Casibari Café, **13**

Coco Plum, **11**

Cuba's Cookin', **6**

Driftwood, **4**

El Gaucho Argentine Grill, **10**

Gostoso, **12**

Kowloon, **1**

L.G. Smith's Steak & Chop House, **3**

The Old Fisherman, **2**

Pinchos Grill & Bar, **9**

Que Pasa?, **5**

West Deck, **8**

Where to Eat in Oranjestad

ORANJESTAD AND ENVIRONS

$$$ ✕ **Arubaville.** *Caribbean.* A fun, colorful, laid-back, beach bar–type joint is a great place to gather for drinks and, come evening, food as well. The make-your-own salad has a nice selection of ingredient choices, and the rack of lamb and seafood platters are served with big appetites in mind. There are a few vegetarian choices on the menu as well. Live music most weekends keeps things hopping, and board games and hammocks make this a favorite for day-trippers. Come at sunset for wonderful views. ⑤ *Average main: $25* ✉ *Bucutiweg 50, Oranjestad* ☎ *297/582–0157* ⊕ *www.arubaville.aw.*

★ **Fodor's**Choice ✕ **Barefoot.** *Contemporary.* In keeping with an

$$ "elegant dining in flip-flops" concept, Barefoot is a palapa restaurant with sand on the floor inside, and tables on the sand outside. Chef Gerco Aan het Rot and maître d'–sommelier Luc Beerepoot excel at pairing food and wine or cocktails. Their menu of creative international fusion cuisine is complemented by superb signature cocktails and an impressive selection of wines, yet the atmosphere is never stuffy. This duo truly takes it up a notch above your basic toes-in-the-sand dining spot, and the sunset views are always spectacular. ⑤ *Average main: $26* ⊠ *L. G. Smith Boulevard 1, across the street from the talk of the Town Hotel on Surfside Beach, Oranjestad* ☎ *297/588–9824* ⊕ *www. barefootaruba.com* ⚓ *Reservations essential* ☺ *No lunch.*

$$ ✕ **Casibari Cafe.** *Barbecue.* The bizarre Flintstone bedrock-style rock formations at Casibari make a great backdrop to this casual, offbeat restaurant where wood-fired barbecue is king. The lunch menu is small, with only a few soups, salads, and sandwiches, all of which are delicious. They fire up the grill for dinner—the mixed grill portions are generous, and the coleslaw side is delicious. Seating is strictly alfresco. After dark the rocks are playfully illuminated for the nighttime crowd—this is a regular stop for the Kukoo Kunuku party bus. ⑤ *Average main: $15* ⊠ *Casibari, Paradera* ☎ *297/586– 1775* ⊕ *www.casibaricafe.com* ☺ *Closed Sun.*

★ **Fodor's** Choice   ✕ **Cuba's Cookin'.** *Cuban.* Old Havana meets the
$$$ Caribbean here with authentic music and food from what locals call "The Big Island." The signature dish is the *ropa vieja,* a sautéed flank steak served with a rich sauce—it's perfectly spiced and melts in your mouth. Vegetarian and gluten-free offerings are served as well. And their boast of the "the best mojitos in town" is a fair claim. There's live music some nights as well as interesting offerings like Poetry Night where locals get up and express themselves through spoken word. The atmosphere is fun and friendly and the location ideal for people-watching along the seaport marina. And it's the only place in town to get a famous Cuban sandwich for lunch. ⑤ *Average main: $28* ⊠ *Renaissance Marketplace, L. G. Smith Blvd. 82, Oranjestad* ☎ *297/588–0627* ⊕ *www.cubascookin.com.*

$$$$ ✕ **Driftwood.** *Caribbean.* Charming owner Francine Merryweather greets you at the door of this Aruban institution, which resembles a series of fishermen's huts. Her husband Herby sets out in his boat every morning, as he has since the late 1980s, to bring the freshest ingredients back to the kitchen. Order his catch prepared as you like—Aruban-style (panfried with a fresh tomato, vegetable, and local herbs) is best—or another of the fine fish dishes. The fish soup is based on a family recipe and has been a staple on the menu for more than 25 years. If you book a fishing trip with their company Driftwood Charters, the chef will also cook up your catch for your dinner. ⑤ *Average main: $31* ⊠ *Klipstraat 12, Oranjestad* ☎ *297/583–2515* ⊕ *www. driftwoodaruba.com* ☺ *Closed Sun.*

Most Aruba restaurants are casual and fun places for a drink and a meal.

$$$$ ✕ **El Gaucho Argentine Grill.** *Steakhouse.* Faux-leather-bound
FAMILY books, tulip-top lamps, wooden chairs, and tile floors deco-
rate this Argentina-style steakhouse, which has been in
business since 1977. The key here is meat served in mam-
moth portions (think 16-ounce steaks), and the "biggest
shish kebab ever served" is also their specialty. But it's
not all about meat: their seafood platters are something
to consider as well. It's a boisterous and fun atmosphere
with strolling musicians, and the kids will enjoy the separate children's playroom. Appropriate attire is appreciated.
Ⓢ *Average main: $40* ✉ *Wilhelminastraat 80, Oranjestad*
☎ *297/582–3677* ⊕ *www.elgaucho-aruba.com.*

$$ ✕ **14-Bis Marketplace.** *International.* This is a good choice for
breakfast, lunch, or an early dinner (they close at 6 pm) if
you need to be at the Queen Beatrix airport. The people
at 14-bis have hit on a winning concept: food is sold by
the kilo ($2.25 per 100 grams) from a large market-style
buffet that serves hot and cold dishes. They're just outside
the security gate and offer healthful to-go options that are
more gently priced than the restaurants inside the terminal.
Free Wi-Fi is also a plus. Ⓢ *Average main: $15* ✉ *Queen
Beatrix International Airport, Oranjestad* ☎ *297/588–1440.*

$$$ ✕ **Gostoso.** *Caribbean.* Locals adore the magical mixture of
Portuguese, Aruban, and international dishes on offer at
this consistently excellent establishment. The décor walks
a fine line between kitschy and cozy, but the atmosphere
is relaxed and informal and outdoor seating is available.

The *bacalhau vinaigrette* (dressed salted cod) is a delightful Portuguese appetizer and pairs nicely with most of the Aruban dishes on the menu. Meat-lovers are sure to enjoy the Venezuelan mixed grill, which includes a 14-ounce steak and chorizo accompanied by local sides like fried plantain. Service is very attentive and a table visit from the owner is par for the course. ⑤ *Average main: $30* ✉ *Caya Ing Roland H. Lacle 12, Oranjestad* ☎ *297/588–0053* ⊕ *www.gostoso aruba.com* ⌗ *Reservations essential* ⊘ *Closed Mon.*

$$$ ✕**Kowloon.** *Asian.* Don't be put off by the dull exterior or off-the-beaten-track location of this fine Asian establishment. The interior décor is tasteful and relaxing, and the combination of Indonesian and authentic Chinese is truly inspired. The most interesting items are in the Epicurean Tour of China section of the menu. The Setju Hoi Sin (the house specialty), a combination of seafood, green pepper, and black beans, is fiery but satisfying. ⑤ *Average main: $23* ✉ *Emmastraat 11, Oranjestad* ☎ *297/582–4950* ⊕ *www.kowloonaruba.com.*

★ Fodor'sChoice ✕**L. G. Smith's Steak & Chop House.** *Steakhouse.* A
$$$$ study in teak, cream, and black, this fine steakhouse offers some of the best beef on the island. Subdued lighting and cascading water create a pleasant atmosphere, and the view over L. G. Smith Boulevard to the harbor makes for an exceptional dining experience. Their comprehensive wine list has won a *Wine Spectator* Award of Excellence. The menu features high-quality cuts of meat, all superbly prepared. The casino is steps away if you fancy some slots after dinner. Nightcaps can be had at the trendy bar Blu just below. ⑤ *Average main: $37* ✉ *Renaissance Aruba Beach Resort & Casino, L. G. Smith Blvd. 82, Oranjestad* ☎ *297/523–6195* ⊕ *www.lgsmiths.com* ⊘ *No lunch.*

$$$ ✕**The Old Fisherman.** *Seafood.* Although it's not the fanciest place, this downtown institution is popular with locals and is always a good bet for excellent seafood. The catch of the day never disappoints, and neither does the grilled conch, if it's available. The more ambitious can try the 2.2 pounds of fried shrimp. Meat dishes here are not as consistent as the seafood. The sides are basic but filling, and almost every main course comes with fries, rice, and coleslaw. It also does a brisk lunch and breakfast business with locals. ⑤ *Average main: $21* ✉ *Havenstraat 36, Oranjestad* ☎ *297/588–3648* ⊕ *www.oldfishermanaruba.com.*

★ Fodor'sChoice ✕**Pinchos Grill & Bar.** *Eclectic.* Built on a pier, this
$$$ casual spot with only 16 tables has one of the most romantic settings on the island. At night the restaurant glimmers from a distance as hundreds of lights reflect off the water.

CLOSE UP

Aruba's Spicy Cuisine

Arubans like their food spicy, and that's where the island's famous Madame Janette sauce comes in handy. It's made with Scotch bonnet peppers (similar to habanero peppers), which are so hot, they can burn your skin when they're broken open. Whether they're turned into *pika*, a relishlike mixture made with papaya, or sliced thin into vinegar and onions, these peppers are sure to set your mouth ablaze. Throw even a modest amount of Madame Janette sauce into a huge pot of soup, and your taste buds will tingle. (Referring to the sauce's spicy nature, Aruban men often refer to an attractive woman as a "Madame Janette.")

To tame the flames, don't go for a glass of water, as capsaicin, the compound in peppers that produces the heat, isn't water soluble. Dairy products (especially), sweet fruits, and starchy foods such as rice and bread are the best remedies.

The restaurant's name comes from the Spanish word for a skewered snack so there are always a few of those on the menu. Guests can watch as the chef prepares delectable meals on the grill in his tiny kitchen while owners, Anabela and Robby, keeps diners comfortable and happy. The fish-cakes appetizer with a pineapple-mayonnaise dressing is a marriage made in heaven. The bar area is great for enjoying ocean breezes over one of their excellent signature cocktails or artisanal sangrias, and sometimes there's live entertainment. Magical at night is the lit-up water below the tables where you can see the colorful fish swimming by. Romance is always on tap here, especially with the lover's swing by the bar. ⑤ *Average main: $24* ⊠ *L. G. Smith Blvd. 7, Oranjestad* ☎ *297/583–2666* ⊗ *No lunch.*

$$$ ✕ **Qué Pasa?**. *Eclectic.* This funky eatery serves as something of an art gallery–restaurant where diners can appreciate the colorful, eclectic works of local artists while enjoying a meal or savoring a drink. The terra-cotta outdoor spaces are illuminated by strings of lights. Inside, jewel-color walls serve as an eye-popping backdrop for numerous paintings. Despite the name, there isn't a Mexican dish on the menu, which includes sashimi, rack of lamb, and fish dishes (they are especially good). Everything is done with Aruban flair, the staff are helpful and friendly, and creative chef specials change daily. It's also a great spot to stop in for signature cocktails and special tapas, and they have special evenings like Sushi Night to watch for. ⑤ *Average main: $22* ⊠ *Wilhelminastraat*

18, Oranjestad ☎ 297/583–4888 ⊕ www.quepasaaruba.com ⊘ No lunch.

$$ ✕**The West Deck.** *Caribbean.* Opened by the same people who own Pinchos, this new fun, friendly, wooden-decked grill joint offers casual fare like barbecue ribs and grilled shrimp by the dozen, as well as Caribbean bites like jerk wings, fried *funchi* (like a thick polenta) with Dutch cheese, and West Indian samosas. There are some surprisingly snazzy dishes too: the lobster/crab cocktail with red grapefruit and cognac cream drizzle is lovely. Their Beer-Ritas (a full bottle of beer served upside down in a big glass of margarita) are becoming legendary. Located at the base of the new Linear Park, it's the perfect place for sunset views over the ocean as the cruise ships come and go. ⑤ *Average main: $15* ⊠ *L. G. Smith Blvd. at Governor's Bay, Oranjestad* ☎ 297/587–2667 ⊕ www.thewestdeck.com.

$$$ ✕**Waka Waka Safari Restaurant.** *Caribbean.* Themed with an African motif that includes zebra-skin décor and safari-suited servers, this family-run spot serves local Caribbean dishes with an African twist. The ribs with Mozambique rub and South African lobster tails are good, but the *machi betti's* (chicken wings with a creole peanut sauce), and Grandma's barbecue platter with tiger rice and Congo coleslaw are real showstoppers. Start with a snack of cheetah chips (crunchy fried plantains with Thai peanut sauce) and an exotic cocktail from the excellent drink list. ⑤ *Average main: $23* ⊠ *Schotlandstraat 61, Oranjestad* ☎ 297/582–5600 ⊕ www.waka wakaaruba.com ⌂ *Reservations essential* ⊘ *Closed Mon.*

MANCHEBO AND DRUIF BEACHES

$$$ ✕**French Steakhouse & Omakase Sushi Bar.** *Steakhouse.* A classic French restaurant with a modern sushi bar under the same roof in a landmark Aruba hotel might sound like a spot with something of an identity crisis, but it actually works. Well known as a place for high-end steak served with European flare, the recent addition of the Asian offerings brings the entire dining room into this century. The Omakase name of the sushi bar means "I will leave it to you," and you are expected to leave it to the sushi chef to delight you with the selection of dishes beginning with the lightest to the heaviest. Seating is limited so reservations at the sushi bar are essential. The French Steakhouse also offers an early-bird menu. Live piano music adds to the ambience. ⑤ *Average main: $30* ⊠ *Manchebo Beach Resort,*

J. E. Irausquin Blvd. 55, Manchebo Beach ☎297/582–3444 ☉ *Sushi bar closed Mon. No lunch.*

$$$$ ✕**Windows on Aruba.** *International.* Sunset views over the greens to the ocean beyond, live music, and impeccable service make this restaurant in the clubhouse of the Divi golf course one of the most romantic spots on the island. Menu items include the usual seafood and meat assortment but are exquisitely prepared and beautifully presented. The cauliflower and truffle soup—an excellent starter— reveals an understanding of turning simple ingredients into a complex taste experience. An excellent à la carte brunch experience with unlimited champagne draws locals and visitors alike every Sunday as well. ⑤ *Average main: $36* ⌂ *Divi Village Golf Resort, J. E. Irausquin Blvd. 41, Divi Beach* ☎297/730–5017 ⊕*www.windowsonaruba.com* ⚓ *Reservations essential* ☉ *No lunch Sat.*

EAGLE BEACH

★ Fodor'sChoice ✕**Elements.** *Contemporary.* A stellar new spot with **$$$$** stunning seaside views of gorgeous Eagle Beach, Bucuti & Tara Beach Resort's Elements embodies their reputation for promoting green living and a healthy lifestyle. Those with dietary restrictions will appreciate the choice of four distinct menus: natural and organic; vegan and vegetarian; gluten-free; and world cuisine. Locally sourced whenever possible is a given. Healthful never equals bland—the menu features imaginative dishes like grilled mango-chili-painted salmon with a coconut butter hollandaise or pineapple stuffed with sautéed quinoa and vegetables and flamed with rum, as well as other interesting takes on seafood and meat. Choose from a three-course tasting menu with organic wine options. The iPad menu in five languages is a nice touch. Note that there is no added gratuity, which is unusual. This is an adults-only (18+), credit card–only establishment—kids and cash are best left at home. ⑤ *Average main: $40* ⌂ *L. G. Smith Blvd. 55B, Eagle Beach* ☎297/583–1100 ⊕*www.elementsaruba.com* ⚓ *Reservations essential.*

$$ ✕**Hollywood Smokehouse.** *Barbecue.* Southern-style barbecue meets Caribbean hospitality at this casual eatery in the Alhambra Casino Shopping Arcade. Wicker baskets with checked paper and picnic-style plastic tablecloths set the stage for their melt-in-your-mouth, low-and-slow-cooked meats, like Carolina-style pulled pork, baby back ribs, and Texas-influenced beef brisket. Fish tacos and chicken-fried steak and gravy round out the menu. Sides include coleslaw, baked beans, and potato salad. Their bar offerings are delicious. Don't miss their signature Bourbonwood Blackberry Lemonade or the interesting Pineapple Arugula Smash. All are mixed with fresh juices, herbs, and house-made syrups. This is the place to catch an American football game, and sometimes they have rollicking live music. ⑤ *Average main: $15* ⊠ *Alhambra Mall, J. E. Irausquin Blvd. 47, Eagle Beach* ☎ *297/280–9989* ⌂ *Reservations essential* ⊗ *No lunch weekdays.*

$$$$ ✕ **The Kitchen Table by White.** *Contemporary.* At perhaps one of the most exciting restaurants on the island, Chef Urvin Croes takes traditional Caribbean dishes, deconstructs them, and then reconstructs them in new and inventive ways. The Kitchen Table seats only 16 people, and the seven-to-eight-course dinner (with optional wine pairing) is served over a four-hour period. The evening kicks off with a sunset cocktail on the patio and then moves to the open kitchen, where diners are close to the action—Chef Croes provides an excellent explanation of each course. Dishes are consistently creative, and the fusion of flavors and unparalleled presentation makes each course a feast. The menu changes monthly, and those with dietary restrictions are absolutely welcome. ⑤ *Average main: $99* ⊠ *The Blue Residence, J. E. Irausquin Blvd. 266, Eagle Beach* ⊕ *www. thekitchentablebywhite.com* ⌂ *Reservations essential.*

$$$$ ✕ **Mango's.** *International.* The main dining spot at Amsterdam Manor is a casual alfresco affair that showcases international dishes and entertainment with different theme nights. Different cuisines are highlighted those nights, such as Italian, French, Mexican, and Asian, but it's their Tuesday Caribbean Buffet and Dance revue that really kicks it up a notch and attracts a regular crowd of guests and locals alike to a fun, alfresco, carnival-like night. They also serve breakfast. ⑤ *Average main: $32* ⊠ *Amsterdam Manor, J. E. Irausquin Blvd. 252, Eagle Beach* ☎ *297/527–1125* ⊕ *www. mangos-restaurant-aruba.com.*

$$$$ ✕ **Passions on the Beach.** *Caribbean.* Every night the Amsterdam Manor Beach Resort transforms the area of Eagle Beach in front of the hotel into a magical and romantic beach dining room. Tiki torches illuminate the white sand, and the linen-covered tables are within inches of the lapping water. Dine on imaginative dishes that are as beautiful as they are delicious. The huge tropical watermelon salad presented in a watermelon half is refreshing and whets the appetite with a slight chili heat. In this "reef cuisine," the main courses lean toward seafood, though meat-lovers also are indulged. After dinner, relax with your toes in the sand and enjoy the best show that nature has to offer over signature cocktails. ⑤ *Average main: $32* ⊠ *Amsterdam Manor Beach Resort, J. E. Irausquin Blvd. 252, Eagle Beach* ☎ *297/527–1100* ⊕ *www.passions-restaurant-aruba. com* ⚄ *Reservations essential.*

$$$$ ✕ **Screaming Eagle.** *French.* The perfect spot for a romantic evening, this elegant French eatery serves creative combinations of fusion cuisine, innovative cocktails, and selections from its generous wine list. The décor is both sophisticated and relaxed, with dramatic triangular sails shading the patio, and soft lighting and billowing draperies inside. Menu items are decidedly French, and each plate is prepared like a mini work of art. For an indulgent experience ask to dine on one of the canopy beds and lounge like an emperor. The Dover sole is prepared tableside (or bedside) à la meunière (lightly floured and sautéed) and makes for a great photo-op. Crêpes Suzette are also prepared tableside. Explore some of the signature or specialty cocktails, like the apple cinnamon mojitos. They're some of the best on the island. ⑤ *Average main: $33* ⊠ *J. E. Irausquin Blvd. 228, Eagle Beach* ☎ *297/587–8021* ⊕ *www. screaming-eagle.net* ⊗ *No lunch.*

$$ ✕ **Tulip.** *International.* Despite the decidedly Dutch name, the global menu features dishes from all over the world, including Indonesian, Arabic, and French favorites. Despite its home in the budget MVC Eagle Beach hotel, the quality is top notch and the service is friendly and relaxed. The Tulip's catch of the day is almost always grouper, and it's excellent, as is the chicken satay and the stick-to-your-ribs Aruban *keshi yena* (stuffed cheese). ⑤ *Average main: $17* ⊠ *J. E. Irausquin Blvd. 240, Eagle Beach* ☎ *297/587–0110* ⊕ *www.tulip-restaurant-aruba.com* ⊗ *Closed Tues.*

PALM BEACH AND NOORD

★ Fodor'sChoice ✕ **Amuse Bistro.** *Contemporary.* The chef-owner
$$$ at Amuse Bistro provides creative French-inspired fusion cuisine, sometimes available in full and small portions, while his sommelier wife will help pair perfect choices of wine from their extensive selection. Pretention, however, is not on the menu here; it's a friendly spot where you can dine outside along Aruba's busiest tourist boulevard or inside in a warm and inviting enclave. The main menu offers mostly classic French dishes with surprising twists, but you're really better served to let the chef delight you with his daily three- or five-course carte blanche surprise menu that can also be paired with the sommelier's choice of wines. The carte blanche menu

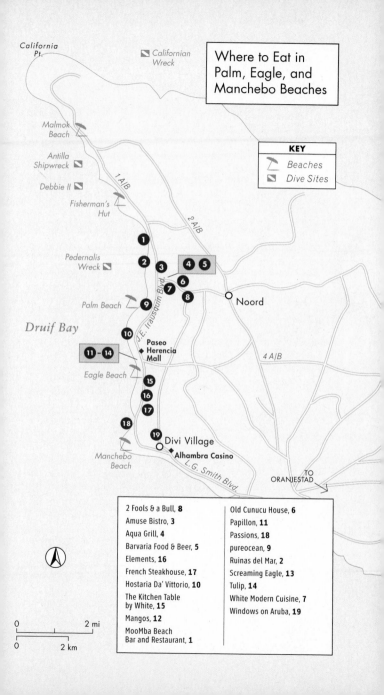

Where to Eat in Palm, Eagle, and Manchebo Beaches

California Pt.

☒ *Californian Wreck*

Malmok Beach

Antilla Shipwreck ☒

Debbie II ☒

Fisherman's Hut

1 A/B

2 A/B

Pedernalis Wreck ☒

①

② **③** **④** **⑤**
        ⑥
      ⑦ **⑧**

○ *Noord*

Palm Beach **⑨**

Druif Bay

⑩

♦ Paseo Herencia Mall

⑪ – ⑭

4 A/B

Eagle Beach **⑮**

⑯

⑰

⑱

⑲ Divi Village
♦ Alhambra Casino

Manchebo Beach

L.G. Smith Blvd.

TO ORANJESTAD

KEY
◞ *Beaches*
☒ *Dive Sites*

0		2 mi
0		2 km

2 Fools & a Bull, **8**
Amuse Bistro, **3**
Aqua Grill, **4**
Barvaria Food & Beer, **5**
Elements, **16**
French Steakhouse, **17**
Hostaria Da' Vittorio, **10**
The Kitchen Table by White, **15**
Mangos, **12**
MooMba Beach Bar and Restaurant, **1**

Old Cunucu House, **6**
Papillon, **11**
Passions, **18**
pureocean, **9**
Ruinas del Mar, **2**
Screaming Eagle, **13**
Tulip, **14**
White Modern Cuisine, **7**
Windows on Aruba, **19**

J.E. Irausquin Blvd.

can only be ordered for the whole table, not individually. Ⓢ *Average main: $28* ✉ *J. E. Irausquin Blvd. 87, Palm Beach* ☎ *297/596–9949* ⚑ *Reservations essential.*

$$$$ ✕ **Aqua Grill.** *Seafood.* Aficionados flock here to enjoy a wide selection of seafood and one of the largest raw bars on the island. The atmosphere is casual, with a distinctly New England feel. Maine lobster and Alaskan king crab legs are available, but why try the usual fare when you can order the Fisherman's Pot, which is filled with scallops, monkfish, and other seafood? The wood grill serves up great low-cal dishes, including mahimahi. There are cheaper restaurants that serve better-prepared seafood meals on the island, but the variety of offerings here sets it apart. Ⓢ *Average main: $32* ✉ *J. E. Irausquin Blvd. 374, Palm Beach* ☎ *297/586–5900* ⊕ *www.aqua-grill.com* ⊗ *No lunch.*

$$ ✕ **Bavaria Food & Beer.** *German.* Those craving bratwurst and sauerkraut during their tropical vacation need worry no more. A variety of German beers, schnitzel, and a true beer-hall feel guarantee to provide that Oktoberfest feeling. The food is hearty and authentic, but if a bit more atmosphere is needed, the wall of cuckoo clocks is sure to fill the bill. With a bright blue exterior and pennants flapping in the breeze, the place is hard to miss. Ⓢ *Average main: $17* ✉ *Palm Beach 186, Palm Beach* ☎ *297/736–4007* ⊕ *www. bavaria-aruba.com* ⊗ *Closed Sun. No lunch.*

$$$ ✕ **Buccaneer.** *Eclectic.* Imagine you're in a sunken ship where FAMILY sharks, barracudas, and grouper swim past the (rectangular) portholes. That's what you can find at Buccaneer, a restaurant dominated by a 10,000-gallon aquarium and where each table has its own individual aquarium. Your best bet is the catch of the day or the rotating chef's special, but there is much more than fish and seafood. It's a great place for kids, and adults will also enjoy their new signature cocktail menu. The restaurant is a landmark family-run establishment that has been operating for more than 30 years. Ⓢ *Average main: $29* ✉ *Gasparito 11C, Noord* ☎ *297/586–6172* ⊕ *www.buccaneer aruba.com* ⊗ *Closed Sun. No lunch.*

★ Fodor's Choice ✕ **Gasparito Restaurant & Art Gallery.** *Carib-*
$$$ *bean.* You can find this enchanting hideaway in a beautifully restored 200-year-old cunucu house in Noord. Dine indoors, where works by local artists are showcased on softly lit walls, or on the outdoor patio. Either way, the service is excellent. Aruban specialties like pan bati and keshi yena come from centuries of tradition and the standout dish is the Gasparito chicken; the sauce recipe was passed down from the owner's ancestors and features seven special

The Goods on Gouda

CLOSE UP

Each year Holland exports more than 250,000 tons of cheese to more than 100 countries, and Gouda (the Dutch pronounce it *how*-da) is one of the most popular. Gouda, named for the city where it's produced, travels well and gets harder, saltier, and more flavorful as it ages. There are six types of Gouda: young (at least 4 weeks old), semi-major (8 weeks old), major (4 months old), ultra-major (7 months old), old (10 months old), and vintage (more than a year old). When buying cheese in shops in Aruba, look for the control seal that confirms the name of the cheese, its country of origin, its fat content, and that it was officially inspected.

4

---

ingredients, including brandy, white wine, and pineapple juice. (The rest, they say, are secret.) Vegetarian entrées and American-style ribs round out the menu of local dishes that include fresh fish and seafood. Only 20 guests are seated per evening—at 6, 7, or 8 pm. ⑤ *Average main: $25* ⌂ *Gasparito 3, Noord* ☎ *297/594–2550* ⊕ *www.gasparito. com* ⌂ *Reservations essential* ⊗ *Closed Sun. No lunch.*

$$$ ✕ **Hostaria Da' Vittorio.** *Italian.* At one of Aruba's most celebrated Italian eateries, part of the fun at this family-oriented spot is watching chef Vittorio Muscariello prepare authentic Italian regional specialties in his open kitchen. The staff helps you choose wines from the extensive list and recommends portions of hot and cold antipasti, risottos, and pastas. Those on a tight budget should stick to the pizza offerings. As you leave, pick up some limoncello (lemon liqueur) or olive oil at the gourmet shop. Be aware that the decibel level of the crowd can be high and service can be slow at peak hours. ⑤ *Average main: $28* ⌂ *L. G. Smith Blvd. 380, Palm Beach* ☎ *297/586–3838* ⊕ *www.hostariavittorio.com.*

★ **Fodor's**Choice ✕ **Madame Janette.** *European.* Named after the

$$$$ Scotch Bonnet pepper (called Madame Janette in Aruba), the food here is surprisingly not Caribbean spicy but French-inspired from the classic haute cuisine–trained chef. Though they do fuse Caribbean flavors when they see fit, especially in the fish and seafood dishes, you'll find a lot of classic heavy butter-and-cream-sauce offerings for the meats like au poivre, béarnaise, and hollandaise. They also have Aruba's largest selection of specialty beers due to one co-owner's avid interest in craft brewing. They also

Jumbo shrimp are a delicious staple at Madame Janette.

have a surprising number of specialty schnitzels. The commitment of the owners to serve only top quality in all of their offerings has won Madame Janette many prestigious culinary awards. You can be sure that a night at this spot will never disappoint when it comes to an over-the-top taste experience. ⑤ *Average main: $33* ✉ *Cunucu Abao 37, Noord* ☎ *297/587–0184* ⊕ *www.madamejanette.info* ⌂ *Reservations essential* ☉ *Closed Sun. No lunch.*

$$$ ✕ **MooMba Beach Bar & Restaurant.** *American.* Though it's best known as a party spot, especially Sunday night when all the locals come out to barefoot boogie in the sand to live music or DJs, many don't realize how good the food is here. The dinners under the giant palapa can be very romantic and first-rate. Best bets are the catch of the day, pasta of the day, and the signature shrimp or killer ribs. It's also a fabulous lunch spot—perfect for people-watching along Aruba's busiest beach. The daily breakfast buffet with an unlimited mimosa option is also noteworthy. Sunset happy hours are popular here, with creative tapas like piña colada shrimp and chorizo potato stacks, and the barkeeps are real showmen as well as great mixologists, so don't miss their signature cocktails. ⑤ *Average main: $25* ✉ *J. E. Irausquin Blvd. 230, Palm Beach* ☎ *297/586–5365* ⊕ *www.moombabeach.com.*

$$$ ✕ **Old Cunucu House.** *Caribbean.* Since the mid-1990s executive chef Ligia Maria has delighted diners with delicious homemade meals in a rustic and cozy traditional cunucu

CLOSE UP

Chowing Down Aruban Style

With its pristine white-sand beaches, clear blue waters, and near perfect year-round weather, Aruba is a mecca for vacationers looking for a warm getaway. The island caters to the demanding tourism industry, which has resulted in a mainly resort-food scene. But if you're interested in a taste of something other than standard American fare—something a bit more unique to the Dutch- and Caribbean-influenced island— then you ought to try one of these local treats.

Balashi: After a day at the beach there's nothing better than sipping a nice, cold Balashi, Aruba's national beer and the only beer brewed on the island. The taste of Balashi is comparable to a Dutch pilsner.

Bitterballen: Crispy bite-size meatballs, which are breaded and then deep-fried, make for the perfect savory snack or appetizer. Dip them in a side of mustard, and wash them down with a cold beverage.

Keshi Yena: A traditional Aruban dish made with chicken, beef, or seafood in a rich brown sauce of spices and raisins, keshi yena is served with rice in a hollowed-out Gouda cheese rind.

Funchi: This classic Aruban cornmeal side dish is eaten at all times of day and is commonly served with soup.

Pan Bati: The slightly sweet pancakes are commonly eaten as a side with meat, fish, or soup entrées.

Pan Dushi: Delectable little raisin bread rolls are *dushi*, which is Papiamento for "sweet."

Pastechi: Aruba's favorite fast food is an empanada-like fried pastry filled with spiced meat, fish, or cheese.

Kesio: This popular dessert is essentially a custard flan or crème caramel.

Cocada: Bite-size pieces of these sweet coconut candies are typically served on a coconut shell.

4

---

house. This spot is one of the best on the island for authentic *crioyo* (local) cuisine. Try their version of Aruba's famous keshi yena—chicken, raisins, olives, cashews, peppers, and rice in a hollowed-out Gouda rind—or thick, hearty *stobas* (stews) of goat or beef. The fresh catch of the day with special sauces is a treat, and the stewed conch is also very good. There's live music some nights, giving the place a local party atmosphere. ⑤ *Average main: $21* ⌗ *Palm Beach 150, Palm Beach* ☎ *297/586–1666* ⊕ *www.theoldcunucuhouse. com* ⊗ *Closed Sun.*

$$$$ ✕**Papillon.** *French.* Despite being inspired by Henri Char-
rière's escape from Devil's Island, the food here couldn't be
more removed from bread and water. The owners use the
famous autobiography and film as a metaphor for a culinary
journey to freedom—they transform classic French cuisine
with Caribbean flair. There are whimsical prison touches
throughout the restaurant and especially in the washrooms.
The menu includes classics like beef bourguignon but isn't
afraid to offer more adventurous dishes such as a standout
crispy duck breast served with passion fruit and chocolate,
and game when it is in season like deer and wild boar.
Whatever you order, you'll find that the presentation is
impeccable. ⑤ *Average main: $35* ✉ *J. E. Irausquin Blvd.
348A, The Village, Palm Beach* ☎ *297/586–5400* ⊕ *www.
papillonaruba.com* ⌂ *Reservations essential.*

$$$$ ✕**Papiamento.** *Eclectic.* The Ellis family converted its
126-year-old manor into a bistro with an atmosphere that is
elegant, intimate, and always romantic. You can feast in the
dining room, which is filled with antiques, or outdoors on
the terrace by the pool (sitting on plastic patio chairs covered in fabric). The chef mixes Continental and Caribbean
cuisines to produce sumptuous seafood and meat dishes
and goes out of his way to source locally for fresh ingredients. Those seeking a bit of novelty can order one of the
hot-stone dishes, which come to the table sizzling. Service
is unhurried and the atmosphere laid-back. Papiamento is
one of the best spots on the island to try the famous local
specialty keshi yena. ⑤ *Average main: $32* ✉ *Washington
61, Noord* ☎ *297/586–4544* ⊕ *www.papiamentoaruba.com*
⌂ *Reservations essential* ☙ *Closed Mon. No lunch.*

$$$ ✕**pureocean.** *Contemporary.* Part of the Divi Aruba Phoe-
nix Beach Resort, pureocean has an excellent selection of
international dishes, an extensive cocktail menu, and one
of the most romantic settings on the island. Come at sunset,
dig your toes into the sand, and dine right on the beach at a
tiki torch–lighted seaside table, or choose a spot under the
elegant and roomy open-air palapa. Daytime diners can graze
the buffet. In the evening, an à la carte menu might include
starters such as the coconut curry mussels and Bloody Mary
shooters. For the main course, Caribbean mac 'n' cheese
(with lobster) and the coconut-curry grouper are excellent.
Finish off with a warm molten chocolate bread pudding and
a little something from the well-stocked bar. ⑤ *Average main:
$25* ✉ *J. E. Irausquin Blvd. 75, Palm Beach* ☎ *297/586–6066*
⊕ *www.diviresorts.com/pure-restaurants.htm* ⌂ *Reservations
essential.*

★ Fodors Choice ✕ **Quinta del Carmen.** *Dutch.* Quinta del Carmen is
$$$$ set in a beautifully restored 100-year-old mansion with stunning manicured lawns and a lovely outdoor courtyard. The cuisine here is best defined as modern Caribbean-Dutch with a few traditional Dutch favorites, like cheese croquettes and mushrooms and cream, appearing on the menu as "Grandma's favorites." The watermelon salad is sweet, salty, and perfectly refreshing, and the *sucade-lappen* (flank steak stewed in red wine and herbs) has a depth of flavor that comes from hours in the pot. End the meal with a *stroopwaffel* parfait and something from the generous cocktail menu. Seating in the courtyard is sometimes taken over by wedding parties, so it's best to call ahead. ⑤ *Average main: $35* ⊠ *Bubali 119 Aruba, Noord* ☏ *297/587–7200* ⊕ *www.quintadelcarmen. com* ⌂ *Reservations essential* ⊘ *No lunch.*

$$$$ ✕ **Ruinas del Mar.** *Caribbean.* Meaning "ruins by the sea," this scenic spot is the focal point of the grand dame Hyatt Regency hotel, famous for its gorgeous tropical grounds and water circuit of falls and pools leading to the sea. The trademark black swans swimming around the koi pond cresting the tiki torch–lit terrace of the dining room make for a very romantic setting, and the interior is elegant and refined. Specialties include stone hearth–cooked items and basic international fare that changes at the chef's fancy and with the seasons. Not to be missed is the local pumpkin soup with coconut milk and cilantro. The Sunday champagne brunch buffet is also very popular, and the setting is unparalleled for breakfast weekdays as well. ⑤ *Average main: $39* ⊠ *Hyatt Regency Aruba Beach Resort & Casino, J. E. Irausquin Blvd. 85, Palm Beach* ☏ *297/586–1234* ⊕ *www.aruba.hyatt.com* ⌂ *Reservations essential* ⊘ *No lunch; no dinner Sun.*

$$ ✕ **Simply Fish.** *Caribbean.* Grab a table right on the beach, kick off your shoes, and sink your toes into the powdery sand of Aruba's famed Palm Beach. Aruba Marriott's Simply Fish is a romantic escape that specializes, as the name suggests, in seafood. Tiki torch–lighted, waterside service is welcoming, attentive, and unpretentious. The catch of the day (a choice of five types of fish) is always fresh, seasonal, and sustainable, and the bouillabaisse is an excellent start to the meal. Meat eaters should be aware that they have only two menu options: filet mignon and roasted chicken breast. It's best to reserve a table before sunset for beautiful views. ⑤ *Average main: $40* ⊠ *L. G. Smith Blvd. 101, Noord* ☏ *297/520–6537* ⊕ *www.marriott.com/hotels/hotel-information/restaurant/*

auaar-aruba-marriott-resort-and-stellaris-casino ⌂ *Reservations essential* ⊘ *Closed Wed. No lunch.*

$$$ ✕ **Solanio.** *Modern Italian.* For first-rate Italian food, stellar sunsets, and an unpretentious environment, head to the Ritz-Carlton Aruba's indoor/outdoor Solanio. Large windows allow for lovely views from inside, and alfresco diners are treated to softly played live music, cooling trade winds, and a cheery bonfire. The food is carefully prepared in an open kitchen, and the atmosphere is casual. The smoky braised short ribs make an outstanding start to the meal, and the risotto with wild mushroom and black truffle is woodsy and rich. Pizza and pasta menus have standout gluten-free options. Sunday brunch is becoming very popular. ⑤ *Average main: $25* ⊠ *L. G. Smith Blvd. 107, Noord* ☎ *297/527–2222* ⊕ *www.ritzcarlton.com* ⊘ *No lunch.*

$$$$ ✕ **2 Fools and a Bull.** *International.* Friends Paul and Fred have teamed up to offer an evening of culinary entertainment that's more like a fun dinner party than a mere dining experience. Guests are assembled and introduced to one another. Then the evening's meal is explained before everyone sits down at the U-shaped communal dinner table for a five-course culinary adventure. The menu changes daily, and there's a selection of suggested wine pairings available by the glass. This isn't a cheap dining experience, but it'll certainly be a cherished memory of Aruba. Reservations are advisable at least a few weeks in advance. ■TIP➜ Be sure to state any dietary restrictions in advance. ⑤ *Average main: $90* ⊠ *Palm Beach 17, Noord* ☎ *297/586–7177* ⊕ *www.2foolsandabull.com* ⌂ *Reservations essential* ⊘ *Closed weekends.*

$$$$ ✕ **White Modern Cuisine.** *Contemporary.* The décor here is white, modern, and minimalist—the perfect stage for local chef and owner Urvin Croes's outstanding culinary experiments, like sea bass with shrimp and chorizo risotto, sweet basil coulis, tomato chips, and a creamy tomato Pernod sauce. Everything on the menu is creatively prepared and stunningly presented. Chef Croes isn't shy about taking risks, like adding lionfish (a threat to Aruba's reefs) to the menu as a regular item. Though the location in a mall is not the most conducive to romance, it's hard not to fall in love with this restaurant. ⑤ *Average main: $35* ⊠ *Palm Beach Plaza, L. G. Smith Blvd. 95, Palm Beach* ☎ *297/586–1190* ⊕ *www.whitecuisine.com* ⊘ *Closed Sun. No lunch.*

WESTERN TIP (CALIFORNIA DUNES)

$$$$ ×**Ventanas del Mar.** *Eclectic.* Floor-to-ceiling windows provide ample views across the lovely Tierra del Sol golf course and beyond to rolling sand dunes and the sea and the landmark California Lighthouse. Dining on the open-air terrace amid flickering candles inspires romance. Inside there's a distinctly country-club atmosphere. Sandwiches, salads, conch fritters, nachos, and quesadillas fill the midday menu; at night the emphasis is on seafood and meat. The crispy whole red snapper in a sweet-and-sour sauce and the crab-and-corn chowder are specialties. Ask about their "All-you-can-taste" night and early-bird menu that changes during the week. Before or after dinner, relax in style on their plush couches in their stylish lounge. Ⓢ *Average main: $32* ⊠ *Tierra del Sol Resort, Malmokweg* ☎ *297/586–7800* ⊕ *www.tierradelsol.com/en/ventanas-del-mar-restaurant/ ventanas-del-mar-restaurant* ⊙ *Closed Sun. Apr.–Nov.*

SAVANETA

★ Fodor'sChoice ×**Flying Fishbone.** *Seafood.* This friendly, relaxed
$$$$ beach restaurant is well off the beaten path in Savaneta, a small fishing town, so you know the fish is seriously fresh, often caught that day. You can dine with your toes in the sand (they have hooks for your shoes), or enjoy your meal on the wooden deck. The emphasis here is on fresh seafood—beautifully presented on colorful beds of vegetables—but there are good choices for landlubbers, too like grilled maple-leaf duck breast. The shrimp, shiitake, and blue-cheese casserole is a tried-and-true favorite kept on the menu to keep the regulars happy. For dessert, the chocolate ravioli with poached pear and ice cream is not to be missed. ■TIP→ Arrive early for dinner to get a good table closer to the water. Ⓢ *Average main: $34* ⊠ *Savaneta 344, Savaneta* ☎ *297/584–2506* ⊕ *www.flyingfishbone.com* ⚑ *Reservations essential.*

$$$$ ×**The Old Man & The Sea.** *Caribbean.* Local music celebrity Jonathan Vieira and his artist mother, Osyth Henriquez, have created an open-air restaurant so magical that the food seems almost superfluous. The location requires a cab ride (unless you have a rental car), but the beachfront setting, with tables in the sand, is gorgeous. The menu offers both seafood and the usual steak choices, but there is a distinct Caribbean flavor to almost everything. The spicy Caesar salad and seared catch of the day coated in a tangy papaya

Where to Eat Elsewhere on Aruba

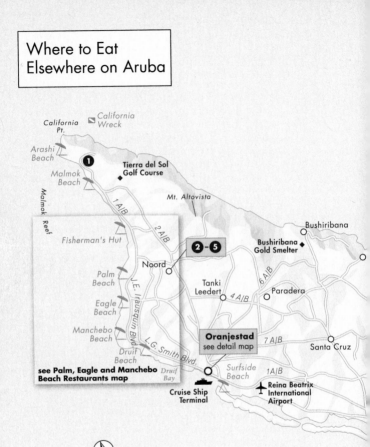

Buccaneer, **2**

Charlie's Restaurant & Bar, **8**

Flying Fishbone, **7**

Gasparito Restaurant & Art Gallery, **3**

Madame Janette's, **4**

The Old Man & The Sea, **6**

Papiamento, **5**

Ventanas del Mar, **1**

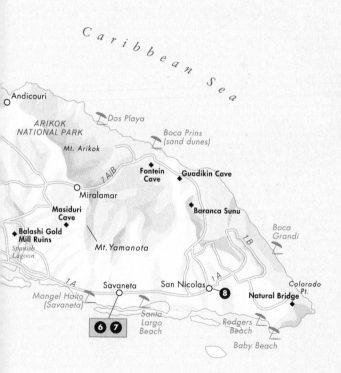

marinade are popular choices. The quality of the food and the service can be erratic, and the prices are high even by Aruban standards. Still, it is hard to get too impatient with sand between your toes. Insect repellent is a must if it's been raining. ⑤ *Average main: $40* ✉ *Savaneta 356A, Savaneta* ☎ *297/735–0840* ⊕ *www.theoldmanandtheseaaruba.com* ⊘ *Closed Sun. No lunch.*

SAN NICOLAS

★ Fodor'sChoice ✕ **Charlie's Restaurant & Bar.** *Caribbean.* For
$$$ almost 75 years of San Nicolas's boom-and-bust oil refinery days, Charlie's Bar has been the town's heart and soul, and it still serves as a magnet for visitors and locals today—it's even run by a third-generation Charlie. Its famous interior—a mini-museum of eclectic items left behind by years of visitors—is only half the attraction; Charlie's serves surprisingly good food for a watering-hole dive. Superb fresh fish and killer steaks have folks trekking out on a regular basis. Charlie's also bottle and sell their own hot Honeymoon Sauce. Lunch or an early dinner are the only options since they close at 7 pm, except for Thursday night when San Nicolas celebrates the weekly Carubbian Festival, a minicarnival in the streets—a perfect opportunity to taste Charlie's signature "Boozer Coladas." ⑤ *Average main: $23* ✉ *Zeppenfeldstraat 56, San Nicolas* ☎ *297/584–5086* ⊘ *Closed Sun. No dinner.*

WHERE TO STAY

THERE'S A GOOD REASON WHY ARUBA has one of the highest repeat-visitor ratios in the Caribbean (some 65% of all first-time visitors return): this island just does tourism right. Beyond the allure of the superb beaches and perfect year-round weather, the level of service and the standards of quality are very high.

Accommodations in Aruba run the gamut from large high-rise hotels and resorts to sprawling time-share condo complexes to small, locally owned boutique establishments and even luxury villa rentals in well-designed private communities where fractional ownership is also an option. Most hotels are west of Oranjestad, along L. G. Smith and J. E. Irausquin boulevards. Many are self-contained complexes, with restaurants, shops, casinos, water-sport centers, health clubs, and spas. And there are a surprising number of small and economical apartment-style hotels, bed-and-breakfasts, and family-run escapes in the interior if you know where to look. All-inclusive options are many, and increasingly, big name-brand hotels are beginning to offer more comprehensive meal plan options. San Nicolas and Savaneta will soon also offer some resorts—one a Zoëtry-brand, upscale, adults-only all-inclusive that will offer South Pacific over-the-water-style bungalows. Time-share has always been big on this island, and the Divi family of resorts offers many different options in their various locations.

The Aruba Tourism Authority honors its repeat guests with a distinguished visitor Ambassador Program. Visitors of 10, 20, and 30 years running receive a certificate and get their photos in the newspaper as part of an appreciation ceremony.

TYPES OF LODGINGS

Almost all the resorts are along the island's southwest coast, along L. G. Smith and J. E. Irausquin boulevards, the larger high-rise properties being farther away from Oranjestad. A few budget places are in Oranjestad itself and in the interior around Noord and Bubali. Since most of Aruba's beaches are equally fabulous, it's the resort, rather than its location, that's going to be a bigger factor in how you enjoy your vacation.

Large Resorts: These all-encompassing vacation destinations offer myriad dining options, casinos, shops, water-sports centers, health clubs, and car-rental desks. The island also has many all-inclusive options.

Best Bets for Lodging

Fodor's offers a selective listing of high-quality lodging experiences, from the island's best boutique hotel to its most luxurious beach resort. Here we've compiled our top recommendations based on the different types of lodging found on the island. The very best properties—in other words, those that offer a particularly remarkable experience—are designated in the listings with the Fodor's Choice logo.

Fodor's Choice: Aruba Marriott Resort & Stellaris Casino; Bucuti & Tara Beach Resorts; Hyatt Regency Aruba Beach Resort & Casino; Renaissance Aruba Resort & Casino; Divi Aruba Beach Resort All Inclusive; Divi Aruba Phoenix Beach Resort; Boardwalk Small Hotel Aruba.

Best Budget Stay: Tropicana Aruba Resort & Casino; MVC Eagle Beach; Bubali Bliss Studios.

Best Boutique Hotel: Bucuti & Tara Beach Resorts; Boardwalk Small Hotel Aruba.

Best High-Rise Resort: Divi Aruba Phoenix Beach Resort; Aruba Marriott Resort & Stellaris Casino; Radisson Aruba Resort & Casino; Holiday Inn Resort Aruba.

Best for Honeymooners: Bucuti & Tara Beach Resorts; Hyatt Regency Aruba Beach Resort & Casino; Manchebo Beach Resort & Spa.

Best for Families: Holiday Inn Resort Aruba; Hyatt Regency Aruba Beach Resort & Casino; Occidental Grand Aruba; Renaissance Aruba Resort & Casino

Time-Shares: Large time-share properties are also popular, luring visitors who prefer to prepare some of their own meals and have a bit more living space than you might find in the typical resort hotel room.

Boutique Resorts: You'll find a few small resorts that offer more personal service, though not always with the same level of luxury as the larger places. But smaller resorts better reflect the natural sense of Aruban hospitality you'll find all over the island. There are some lovely B&Bs as well.

PRICES

Hotel rates are high; to save money, take advantage of airline and hotel packages, or visit in summer when rates are discounted by as much as 40%. If you're traveling with kids, ask about discounts; children often stay for free in their parents' room, though there are age cutoffs.

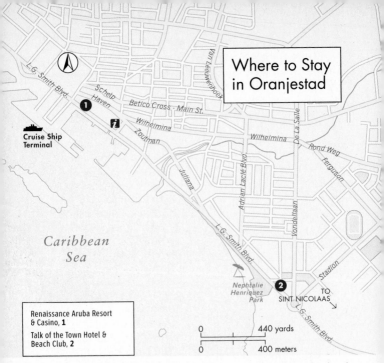

Renaissance Aruba Resort
& Casino, 1

Talk of the Town Hotel &
Beach Club, 2

The following reviews have been condensed for this book. For expanded lodging reviews and current deals, visit Fodors.com.

ORANJESTAD AND ENVIRONS

$$ ☆ **Divi Village Golf & Beach Resort.** *All-Inclusive.* Although it's just across the road from its sister Divi properties, this all-suites version is quieter and more refined. **Pros:** excellent golf course; spacious rooms; lush grounds; free shuttles to sister Divi resorts on the beach; spa has the only hammam on the island. **Cons:** bit of a hike from some rooms to the lobby; it might be a bit too quiet for some; no ocean views. ⑤ *Rooms from: $309* ✉ *J. E. Irausquin Blvd. 93, Oranjestad* ☎ *297/583–5000, 297/583–5000* ⊕ *www.divivillage.com* ⤴ *250 suites* ⑩ *All-inclusive* ⌒ *3-night minimum.*

$ ☆ **Hidden Eden Aruba.** *B&B/Inn.* It's not common knowledge, but there are some very cool little B&Bs on this island, and this is one of the best. **Pros:** affordable; clean; safe; local flavor. **Cons:** not walking distance to beach; not close to shopping; rental car needed. ⑤ *Rooms from: $95* ✉ *Bushiri 12, Oranjestad* ☎ *297/592–5740* ⤴ *4 rooms* ⑩ *Breakfast.*

The Renaissance Aruba's private island

★ **Fodor's**Choice ☒ **Renaissance Aruba Resort & Casino.** *Resort.*
$$$ This landmark property right on the port offers guests the best of both worlds—adults-only accommodations and family-friendly amenities with its own man-made beach. **Pros:** in the heart of the downtown shopping district; lobby and shopping areas are always lively; pool area offers an unmatched view of the port; free access to private island. **Cons:** rooms overlooking the atrium can be a bit claustrophobic; beach is off site; no hotel grounds; no balconies in downtown section; nights can be noisy. ⑤ *Rooms from: $397* ⊠ *L. G. Smith Blvd. 82, Oranjestad* ☎ *297/583–6000, 800/421–8188* ⊕ *www.renaissancearuba.com* ↩ *287 rooms, 269 suites* ⊙ *Multiple meal plans.*

$ ☒ **Talk of the Town Hotel & Beach Club.** *Hotel.* Bright and airy rooms (some with kitchenettes) and excellent rates make this property a great value. **Pros:** great value; close to main shopping area; breakfast included. **Cons:** not luxurious; more of a short-stay hotel; on one of the island's busiest streets; downtown noise. ⑤ *Rooms from: $229* ⊠ *L. G. Smith Blvd. 2, Oranjestad* ☎ *297/582–3380* ⊕ *www.tott aruba.com* ↩ *63 rooms* ⊙ *Breakfast.*

MANCHEBO AND DRUIF BEACHES

$ ▦ **Aruba Beach Club.** *Hotel.* A favorite for families as well as
FAMILY those on a budget, Aruba Beach Club offers basic studios
and one-bedroom units that attract repeat customers who
enjoy a homey getaway on a great beach. **Pros:** family-
friendly atmosphere; great beach; numerous activities;
excellent value. **Cons:** pool area can be very busy; old-
fashioned feel; service is uninspired except in the restaurant. Ⓢ *Rooms from: $200* ✉ *J. E. Irausquin Blvd. 51–53,
Manchebo* ☎ *297/582–3000* ⊕ *www.arubabeachclub.net*
◁ *131 suites* ⦿ *No meals.*

$ ▦ **Casa del Mar Beach Resort.** *Resort.* Deluxe accommodations
FAMILY at this beachside time-share are quite comfortable, with
such amenities as balconies and fully equipped kitchens.
Pros: home-away-from-home feeling; great beach location;
family-friendly. **Cons:** pool area can get crowded; lots of
kids; rooms feel a bit dated; few quiet spots on property.
Ⓢ *Rooms from: $225* ✉ *L. G. Smith Blvd. 53, Manchebo*
☎ *297/582–3000, 297/582–7000* ⊕ *www.casadelmar-aruba.
com* ◁ *147 suites* ⦿ *No meals.*

$$$$ ▦ **Divi Aruba Beach Resort All Inclusive.** *All-Inclusive.* The free
FAMILY food and drinks here and the ability to use the facilities of
the adjoining sister Tamarijn Resort mean you have very
little reason to wander far from the idyllic beach location.
Pros: on wonderful stretch of beach; common areas feel
light and airy; great staff. **Cons:** buffet could use more variety; you must wear bracelets; charge for Wi-Fi. Ⓢ *Rooms
from: $638* ✉ *L. G. Smith Blvd. 93, Manchebo Beach*
☎ *297/582–3300, 800/554–2008* ⊕ *www.diviaruba.com*
◁ *205 rooms, 4 suites* ⦿ *All-inclusive* ⌖ *5-night minimum.*

$ ▦ **Divi Dutch Village.** *Hotel.* A pair of free-form freshwater
pools are at the center of this quiet, oceanfront time-share.
Pros: beautiful beach is just steps away, and supermarkets are within walking distance; quieter than the other
Divi properties on the beach. **Cons:** not directly on the
beach; no ocean views from any rooms; charge for Wi-Fi.
Ⓢ *Rooms from: $235* ✉ *J. E. Irausquin Blvd. 47, Druif
Beach* ☎ *297/583–5000, 800/367–3484* ⊕ *www.dividutch-
village.com* ◁ *97 units* ⦿ *No meals.*

$$ ▦ **Manchebo Beach Resort & Spa.** *All-Inclusive.* One of the
original low-rise resorts on the island, Manchebo Beach
Resort has the broadest beach stretch, with scads of room
for quiet lounging. **Pros:** fabulous beach; casino and shop-
ping only steps away; intimate and personal; lovely land-
scaping. **Cons:** rooms are on the small side; not much in way

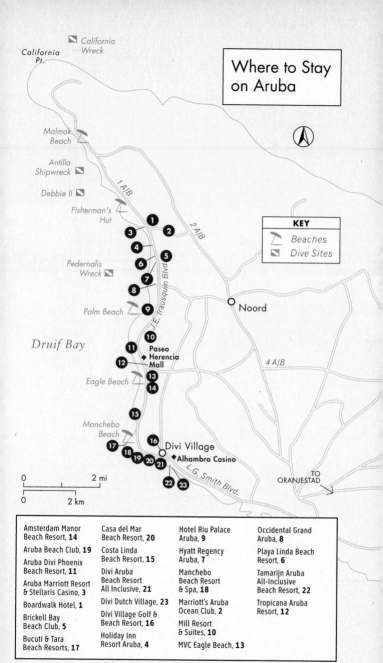

Where to Stay on Aruba

California Pt.

California Wreck

Malmok Beach

Antilla Shipwreck

Debbie II

Fisherman's Hut

Pedernalis Wreck

Palm Beach

Druif Bay

Eagle Beach

Manchebo Beach

KEY
- Beaches
- Dive Sites

1 A|B

2 A|B

4 A|B

Noord

Paseo Herencia Mall

Divi Village

Alhambra Casino

L.G. Smith Blvd.

J.E. Trausquin Blvd.

TO ORANJESTAD

0 — 2 mi
0 — 2 km

Amsterdam Manor Beach Resort, **14**

Aruba Beach Club, **19**

Aruba Divi Phoenix Beach Resort, **11**

Aruba Marriott Resort & Stellaris Casino, **3**

Boardwalk Hotel, **1**

Brickell Bay Beach Club, **5**

Bucuti & Tara Beach Resorts, **17**

Casa del Mar Beach Resort, **20**

Costa Linda Beach Resort, **15**

Divi Aruba Beach Resort All Inclusive, **21**

Divi Dutch Village, **23**

Divi Village Golf & Beach Resort, **16**

Holiday Inn Resort Aruba, **4**

Hotel Riu Palace Aruba, **9**

Hyatt Regency Aruba, **7**

Manchebo Beach Resort & Spa, **18**

Marriott's Aruba Ocean Club, **2**

Mill Resort & Suites, **10**

MVC Eagle Beach, **13**

Occidental Grand Aruba, **8**

Playa Linda Beach Resort, **6**

Tamarijn Aruba All-Inclusive Beach Resort, **22**

Tropicana Aruba Resort, **12**

The beachfront at Bucuti & Tara Beach Resorts

of entertainment. *⑤ Rooms from: $305 ⊠ J. E. Irausquin Blvd. 55, Manchebo Beach ☎ 297/582–3444, 800/223–1108 ⊕ www.manchebo.com ⇔ 72 rooms ⊙ All-inclusive.*

$$$$ 🏨 **Tamarijn Aruba All-Inclusive Beach Resort.** *All-Inclusive.* Sister property of the Divi Aruba Beach Resort All Inclusive, this property is decidedly more laid-back and all rooms are oceanfront on a spectacular beach that is walking distance from town. **Pros:** stunning beach; access to the Divi Aruba Beach Resort All Inclusive next door; nightly entertainment. **Cons:** Wi-Fi is an additional charge; daytime might be too quiet for some. *⑤ Rooms from: $614 ⊠ J. E. Irausquin Blvd. 41, Punta Brabo ☎ 297/594–7888, 800/554–2008 ⊕ www.tamarijnaruba.com ⇔ 216 rooms, 20 suites ⊙ All-inclusive ⇔ 3-night minimum.*

EAGLE BEACH

$ 🏨 **Amsterdam Manor Beach Resort.** *All-Inclusive.* Amsterdam
FAMILY Manor is an intimate, family-run hotel with a genuinely friendly staff, offering excellent value without too many frills. **Pros:** feels like a European village; friendly and helpful staff; minigrocery on site; public bus stop in front of hotel for easy access to downtown and the high-rise area. **Cons:** across the road from the beach; lacks the boutiques and attractions of a larger hotel; small pool; Jet Skis at beach can be noisy. *⑤ Rooms from: $225 ⊠ J. E. Irausquin Blvd.*

252, Eagle Beach ☎297/527–1100, 800/932–2310 ⊕*www. amsterdammanor.com* ⌇*68 rooms, 4 suites* ¦O¦*All-inclusive.*

$$ ☒**Blue Residences.** *Hotel.* Bookended by Aruba's two most famous beaches (Eagle and Palm) on its own private manmade sandy strand right across the street, the new Blue Residence Towers—three columns suites ranging from one to five bedrooms—offer epic unfettered views of the sea. **Pros:** full concierge services; excellent dining; sea views; infinity pool; fitness center; spa. **Cons:** not directly on beach; far walk to shopping; little on-site entertainment. ⑤*Rooms from: $225* ⊠*J. E. Irausquin Blvd. 26, Eagle Beach* ☎297/528–7000 ⊕*www.bluearuba.com* ⌇*120 rooms.*

★ **Fodor'sChoice** ☒**Bucuti & Tara Beach Resorts.** *Hotel.* An extraordinary beach setting, impeccable personal service, and attention to detail help this elegant Green Globe resort easily outclass anything else on the island. **Pros:** sophisticated atmosphere; impeccable service; free self-service laundry; free Wi-Fi throughout; free use of netbooks during stay; outdoor bar is for exclusive use of hotel guests. **Cons:** beach can get busy because other hotels share it; no room service; no longer doing beach weddings. ⑤*Rooms from: $451* ⊠*L. G. Smith Blvd. 55B, Eagle Beach* ☎297/583–1100 ⊕*www.bucuti.com* ⌇*63 rooms, 38 suites, 3 bungalows* ¦O¦*Breakfast.*

$$$ ☒**Costa Linda Beach Resort.** *Resort.* The aptly named "Beautiful Coast" time-share resort crests a gorgeous 600-foot stretch of Eagle Beach. **Pros:** beautiful location; many activities available; great beach. **Cons:** large resort lacks intimacy; kids are everywhere; more expensive than some comparable properties in the area. ⑤*Rooms from: $378* ⊠*J. E. Irausquin Blvd. 59, Eagle Beach* ☎297/583–8000 ⊕*www.costalinda-aruba.com* ⌇*155 suites* ¦O¦*No meals.*

$ ☒**MVC Eagle Beach.** *Hotel.* What started as a vacation facility for the visiting families of Dutch marines is now a great bargain hotel across from Eagle Beach. **Pros:** unbeatable price; free Wi-Fi; short walk to beach; friendly and helpful staff. **Cons:** lacks all the amenities of larger resorts; not for those who want to be away from children. ⑤*Rooms from: $205* ⊠*J. E. Irausquin Blvd. 240, Eagle Beach* ☎297/587–0110 ⊕*www.mvceaglebeach.com* ⌇*16 rooms, 3 suites* ¦O¦*No meals.*

$ ☒**Tropicana Aruba Resort & Casino.** *Resort.* An excellent waterslide, fast-food options, and a nearby supermarket make this complex of self-contained time-share units right across from Eagle Beach a popular choice for families.

Amsterdam Manor Beach Resort, a small hotel on Eagle Beach, is still family-run.

Pros: nice pools and waterfall; supermarket right across the street; price is hard to beat for a hotel so close to the beach. **Cons:** feels like an apartment complex; public areas are noisy and crowded; despite the attractions for children, there are no kids' programs offered. ⓢ *Rooms from: $191* ✉ *J. E. Irausquin Blvd. 250, Eagle Beach* ☎ *297/587–9000, 800/835–7193* ⊕ *www.troparuba.com* 🛏 *362 suites* ❍ *No meals.*

PALM BEACH AND NOORD

★ Fodor'sChoice ⚏ **Aruba Marriott Resort & Stellaris Casino.** *Resort.*
$$$ One of the first landmark resorts on the high-rise beach strip, the Aruba Marriott combines family-fun offerings with romance and business by offering an entirely separate luxury floor. **Pros:** every kind of amenity including full-service spa and beauty salon, large conference center/ballroom; shopping. **Cons:** charge for Wi-Fi beyond lobby; can be boisterous around the pool area; beach can become crowded in high season. ⓢ *Rooms from: $411* ✉ *L. G. Smith Blvd. 101, Palm Beach* ☎ *297/586–9000, 800/223–6388* ⊕ *www.marriott.com* 🛏 *388 rooms, 23 suites* ❍ *No meals.*

★ Fodor'sChoice ⚏ **Boardwalk Small Hotel Aruba.** *Hotel.* A gorgeous
$ luxury boutique oasis in an ex–coconut planation, this family run gem is decorated in bright tropical hues with unique accents supplied by local artists. **Pros:** beautiful grounds and décor; intimate and romantic; highly personal service;

CLOSE UP

Associations That Accommodate

Aruba Hotel & Tourism Association. The Aruba Hotel & Tourism Association (better known as AHATA) was established in 1965 to maintain high standards in the tourism industry. From its original seven hotels, the organization has grown to more than 80 businesses, including restaurants, casinos, stores, tour operators, and airlines. The organization's budget, earmarked to promote Aruba as a travel destination, comes from a 7.5% room tax that funds both it and the newly privatized Aruba Tourism Authority. You can express opinions and register complaints on the Aruba Tourism website (⊕ www.aruba. com). The organization is also involved in anti-littering efforts as part of the Aruba Limpi Committee. ☎ 297/582–2607 ⊕ www.ahata.com.

5

eco-aware operation; free Wi-Fi. **Cons:** not right on the beach; limited views; fair walk from shopping. ⓢ *Rooms from: $250* ⊠ *Bakval 20, Palm Beach* ☎ 297/586–6654 ⊕ *www.boardwalkaruba.com* ⇆ *11 1-bedroom suites, 2 2-bedroom suites* ⓞ *No meals.*

$ ▦ **Brickell Bay Beach Club & Spa Boutique Hotel.** *Hotel.* Right in the heart of the main tourist street behind the Palm Beach high-rise resort strip is this adults-only urban stay with its own hidden pool and courtyard. **Pros:** adults only; free Wi-Fi and calls to North America; reasonable price. **Cons:** noisy, busy area; no ocean views; busy pool. ⓢ *Rooms from: $225* ⊠ *J. E. Irausquin Blvd. 370, Palm Beach* ☎ 297/586–0900 ⊕ *www.brickellbayaruba.com* ⇆ *94 rooms, 4 suites* ⓞ *Breakfast.*

$ ▦ **Bubali Bliss Studios.** *Hotel.* The neighborhood might throw you off a little—it's directly behind Super Food, the island's biggest supermarket, and beside an industrial site—but don't let that stop you from checking out this ideal economical spot within walking distance of famed Eagle Beach. **Pros:** flexible anytime self-check-in and -check-out; free Wi-Fi; Aruba Aloe bathroom products; inviting little pool area with hammocks. **Cons:** front looks onto back door of supermarket; extra charge for single-night stay (minimum is three nights); busy traffic area. ⓢ *Rooms from: $205* ⊠ *Bubali 147, Palm Beach* ☎ 297/587–5262 ⊕ *www.bubali bliss.com* ⇆ *10 rooms* ⓞ *No meals.*

★ Fodor's Choice ▦ **Divi Aruba Phoenix Beach Resort.** *Resort.* With
$$$ incredible views from its high-rise tower, stunning rooms awash in tropical colors and state-of–the-art amenities,

The Aruba Marriott Resort & Stellaris Casino is in the heart of Palm Beach.

and comfortable, homey accommodations, Divi Aruba Phoenix offers something for everyone. **Pros:** beautifully appointed rooms; great beach; privacy from main Palm Beach frenzy; great vibe. **Cons:** children don't always stick to their appointed areas; Jet Skis from nearby operator can be noisy. ⑤ *Rooms from: $414* ✉ *J. E. Irausquin Blvd. 75, Palm Beach* ☎ *297/586–1170* ⊕ *www.diviarubaphoenix. com* ⌁ *140 luxury suites, 101 rooms* ⑩ *No meals.*

$$ ⛱ **Holiday Inn Resort Aruba.** *Resort.* Recipient of the 2014 FAMILY "Renovation of the Year" award within the InterContinental Hotels Group Company, this is not your typical Holiday Inn. **Pros:** thematic zones provide distinct amenities; gorgeous pool area with sea views; lively vibe; free Wi-Fi. **Cons:** frequently fully booked; busy pool area; busy reception area. ⑤ *Rooms from: $307* ✉ *J. E. Irausquin Blvd. 230, Palm Beach* ☎ *297/586–3600, 800/465–4329* ⊕ *www. holidayarubaresort.com* ⌁ *597 rooms, 7 suites* ⑩ *Multiple meal plans.*

$$$$ ⛱ **Hotel Riu Palace Aruba.** *All-Inclusive.* This white wedding cake of a resort towers over Palm Beach with one 8-story and two 10-story towers. **Pros:** beautiful vistas; drink dispensers in all rooms; large and lively pool area. **Cons:** pool area and beach is always crowded and loud; constant "spring break" party atmosphere; unimpressive à la carte restaurants; standard Riu interior décor is very out of place for Aruba; nothing locally inspired. ⑤ *Rooms from: $674* ✉ *J. E. Irausquin Blvd. 79, Palm Beach* ☎ *297/586–*

3900, 800/345–2782 ⊕ www.riuaruba.com ↩450 rooms ⎮○⎮ All-inclusive.

★ Fodor'sChoice ⚏ **Hyatt Regency Aruba Beach Resort & Casino.**
$$$$ *Resort.* This 12-acre property is one the most lavishly
FAMILY landscaped resorts on the island, with a glorious array of
bright tropical blooms and lush foliage surrounding a circuit of waterfalls culminating in a koi pond where black
swans glide gracefully by. **Pros:** beautiful grounds; great
for kids; excellent restaurants. **Cons:** small balconies for a
luxury hotel; some rooms are quite a stretch from the beach.
Ⓢ *Rooms from: $650 ⌂ J. E. Irausquin Blvd. 85, Palm Beach*
☎ 297/586–1234, 800/554–9288 ⊕ aruba.hyatt.com ↩342
rooms, 24 suites, 29 regency club rooms ⎮○⎮ *No meals.*

$$$$ ⚏ **Marriott's Aruba Ocean Club.** *Rental.* First-rate amenities
FAMILY and lavishly decorated villas have made this time-share the
island favorite. **Pros:** relaxed atmosphere; feels more like a
home than a hotel room; excellent beach. **Cons:** beach can
get crowded; attracts large families, so kids are everywhere.
Ⓢ *Rooms from: $700 ⌂ L. G. Smith Blvd. 99, Palm Beach*
☎ 297/586–2641 ⊕ www.marriott.com ↩93 *rooms, 213
suites* ⎮○⎮ *No meals.*

$ ⚏ **Mill Resort & Suites.** *Resort.* Quaint yet colorful interiors,
FAMILY a small pool, and a quick shuttle or stroll to one of Aruba's
best beaches make Mill Resort a good choice for families
on a budget. **Pros:** good value; intimate setting; family-
friendly; free Wi-Fi. **Cons:** rooms have limited views and
spare amenities; pool can be crowded with children; not
on beach. Ⓢ *Rooms from: $228 ⌂ J. E. Irausquin Blvd. 330,
Palm Beach* ☎ 297/526–7700 ⊕ www.millresort.com ↩64
studios, 121 suites ⎮○⎮ *Breakfast.*

$$$$ ⚏ **Occidental Grand Aruba Resort & Casino.** *All-Inclusive.* From
the spectacular beach to great nightly entertainment, and
eclectic choice of dining and a dedicated Kids' Club, The
Occidental Grand offers something for everyone. **Pros:**
great beach location; lots of water sports in front; friendly
staff; not spring break–style. **Cons:** nonstop action—few
quiet escape spots; size can make it seem somewhat impersonal at times. Ⓢ *Rooms from: $640 ⌂ J. E. Irausquin Blvd.
83, Palm Beach* ☎ 297/586–4500, 800/448–8355 ⊕ www.
occidentalgrandaruba.com ↩368 *rooms* ⎮○⎮ *All-inclusive.*

$$ ⚏ **Playa Linda Beach Resort.** *Resort.* Playa Linda—one of the
FAMILY island's first time-share options—was designed to look like
a stepped Mayan pyramid, so that the sea views from the
balconies would be optimal. **Pros:** great beach location;
homey rooms; lots of distractions for kids. **Cons:** not all
rooms are up to the same standard; crowded and busy

beachfront. Ⓢ *Rooms from: $315* ✉ *J. E. Irausquin Blvd. 87, Palm Beach* ☎ *297/586–1000* ⊕ *www.playalinda.com* ⌗ *66 studios, 95 1-bedroom suites, 33 2-bedroom suites, 18 townhouses.*

$$ ▨ **Radisson Aruba Resort, Casino & Spa.** *Hotel.* This hotel sits on five acres overflowing with tropical foliage and cresting famous Palm Beach. **Pros:** great location; consistent quality; gorgeous grounds. **Cons:** can feel impersonal; beach can be crowded; lots of children in pool areas. Ⓢ *Rooms from: $390* ✉ *J. E. Irausquin Blvd. 266, Palm Beach* ☎ *297/586-6555* ⊕ *www.radisson.com/palm-beach-hotel-aw/aruaruba* ⌗ *355 rooms* ⑩ *Some meals.*

$ ▨ **Riu Palace Antillas.** *Resort.* In 2014, Riu bought this property, formerly the Westin Hotel, right next door to its other family-friendly Palm Beach all-inclusive, Riu Palace. **Pros:** adults only (18+, and 21+ during spring break season); 24/7 all-inclusive room service; free Wi-Fi. **Cons:** not all rooms have a sea view; beach right next door to busy family Riu; vibe can feel impersonal. Ⓢ *Rooms from: $200* ✉ *J. E. Irausquin Blvd. 77, Palm Beach* ☎ *297/526–4100* ⊕ *www.riu.com/en/Paises/aruba/palmbeach/hotel-riu-palace-antillas* ⌗ *482 rooms* ⑩ *All-inclusive.*

6

NIGHTLIFE AND PERFORMING ARTS

YOU'LL NEVER NEED TO WAIT UNTIL the sun goes down on Aruba to get the party started. The revelry starts early at beach bars and resort happy hours where live music or DJ-driven sounds shake the sunbathers out of their tropical relaxation mode and into barefoot-bopping in the sand. And chances are good on any given week that there will be some kind of day party happening because of one of the many celebrations this island has going on all year long. There are 50-some annual events—carnivals, regattas, sporting competitions, national holiday fêtes, seasonal celebrations, and music, food, wine, and art festivals each year—so whenever you visit, there's bound to be some daytime fun and dancing in the streets or on the beaches.

But once the moon rises and the tiki torches are lighted, you will notice a shift in mood from happy party time to high-octane energy. And if you follow the sounds of music along the high-rise strip or in downtown Oranjestad, you're bound to find a happening that suits your style, be it kicking back in a cozy lounge or dancing 'til dawn. You can easily hop from scene to scene on foot in both places, or take a barhopping bus to discover where the nights really move, along with a wild and crazy crowd. Taxis are easy to find, and the party scene is compact, so there is no need to wander far.

NIGHTLIFE

For information on specific events, check out the free magazines *Aruba Nights, Aruba Experience,* and Island Temptations, all available at the airport and at hotels.

SUNSET CRUISE

Mi Dushi. *Mi dushi* means "my sweetheart" in the local lingo, and this operator has been offering guests snorkeling and sailing trips on Aruban waters for more than three decades. Having recently scuttled their older ship to make a man-made reef, they have a brand-new vessel: a huge, colorful four-deck catamaran than can hold up to 70 people. Tours include music, an open bar, snorkel gear, instruction, and a pirate rope swing. Snorkel tours cover Aruba's three most popular reefs, and romantic sunset sails are also available. You can also charter them for private parties. Excursions depart from the De Palm Pier on Palm Beach. ⊠ *De Palm Pier, Palm Beach* ☎ *297/640–3000* ⊕ *www.midushi.com.*

WEEKLY PARTIES

★ Fodor's Choice **Bon Bini Festival.** This year-round folklore event (the name means "welcome" in Papiamento), is held every Tuesday 6:30 pm–8:30 pm at Fort Zoutman in Oranjestad. In the inner courtyard, you can check out the Antillean dancers in resplendent costumes, feel the rhythms of the steel drums, browse among the stands displaying local artwork, and sample local food and drink. ⊠ *Fort Zoutman, Oranjestad* ⊕ *www.aruba.com* 🖃 *$5.*

ORANJESTAD AND ENVIRONS

BARS

★ Fodor's Choice **BLUE.** Located steps away from the cool infinity pool of the Renaissance Marina Hotel, BLUE is one of the hippest social gathering spots on the island. It's the place where young professional locals gather for happy hour, and it later morphs into a hot DJ-driven scene Thursday through Sunday bathed in blue and violet lights with a giant video wall and talented barkeeps serving upscale concoctions like their signature Blue Solo Martini. And the monthly RLifeLive Event—high-octane entertainment events of Renaissance Hotels worldwide—always takes the party there over the top, often with live bands and special shows. ⊠ *L. G. Smith Blvd. 82, Oranjestad* ☎ *297/583–6000* ⊕ *www. renaissancearubaresortandcasino.com/dining-entertainment/ bars-lounges-en.html.*

★ Fodor's Choice **Eetcafe The Paddock.** It's impossible to miss the big red roof just off the marina, especially since there is a large Holstein cow, a big dinosaur, and an entire car sitting on top of it! But that's the point. Wild, crazy, and whimsical is their claim to fame, and there's no better spot in town to catch Dutch "futball" if you're seeking the craziest orange-clad die-hard fans. Though it's a popular tourist lunch spot during the day, this joint really morphs into party-hearty mode at night, full of carousing locals and visitors alike enjoying the great deals on drinks via the late-night happy hours and dollar-beer specials. Live music often adds to the revelry. ⊠ *L. G. Smith Blvd. 13, Oranjestad* ⊕ *www. paddock-aruba.com.*

Iguana Joe's. The reptilian-themed decor is as colorful and creative as the specialty cocktails served here. A favorite hangout for those who want to enjoy the view of the port from the second-floor balcony. The crowd is primarily tourists during the early evening, and many locals enjoy

6

A sunset happy-hour cruise is a popular pastime.

the laid-back vibe on Friday and Saturday nights. Though famous for their potent drinks, especially their signature Pink Iguana, the food deserves a shout-out as well, especially the jerk chicken and coconut shrimp. ⊠ *Royal Plaza Mall, L. G. Smith Blvd. 94, Oranjestad* ☎ *297/583–9373* ⊕ *www.iguanajoesaruba.com* ☺ *Closed Sun.*

DANCE CLUBS AND MUSIC CLUBS

CILO. Short for "City Lounge," this European-style socializing spot is particularly popular with the Dutch. It's a casual indoor/outdoor gathering venue for bites and meals, including breakfast or cocktails and coffee with friends. They often have live musicians at night as well. Its central location in the Renaissance Marketplace makes it a perfect pit stop after shopping or exploring Oranjestad, and it's a good place to begin a night out downtown. ⊠ *Renaissance Marketplace, L. G. Smith Blvd. 82, Oranjestad* ☎ *297/588–7996* ⊕ *www.CILO-aruba.com.*

Reflextions. Aruba's answer to South Beach is just steps from downtown Oranjestad on Surfside Beach. This upscale hot spot is party central on weekends with the island's hottest DJs and crowds of dancers under techno lights inside and right on the beach. During the day, it's a whole different scene—sleek and sophisticated—with VIP bottle service, an international bites menu, and fancy frozen cocktails. You'll often spot the beautiful people lounging in for-rent cabanas and daybeds or in the massage loungers in the seaside pool. Reflextions offers luggage storage and free transportation to the airport once you've checked out of your hotel if you want a few more hours of beach time before you return home. It's also a very popular spot for private parties, so call ahead to make sure they're open to the public. ⊠ *L. G. Smith Blvd. 2, Oranjestad* ☎ *297/582–0153* ⊕ *www.beach-aruba.com.*

7 West Bar & Restaurant. Named after its address (Westraat 7) this is predominantly an eatery for lunch and casual dinner in the early evening until the lights dim later on to reveal a seriously cool neon glow-in-the-dark interior that attracts a local crowd of thirsty folks seeking signature cocktails amid hot music in downtown Oranjestad. The deck overlooks the harbor, and the new shooter bar underneath it, called Chipotz, gets the party kicking up into high-octane mode even later, especially on weekends. ⊠ *Weststraat 7, Oranjestad* ☎ *297/588–9983* ⊕ *www.7-westaruba.com.*

EAGLE BEACH

BARS/DANCE CLUBS

Pata Pata Bar. The pool deck at La Cabana Resort has a fun swim-up bar where locals and guests go for a festive atmosphere and a two-for-one happy hour daily 4–6 pm and again later 10–11 pm. There's occasional live music. ⊠ *La Cabana All Suite Beach Resort & Casino, J. E. Irausquin Blvd. 250, Eagle Beach* ☎ *297/520–1100* ⊕ *www.lacabana brc.com/food-beverage.*

PALM BEACH AND NOORD

BARS

★ Fodor's Choice **Bugaloe Bar & Grill.** Night and day, this crazy, colorful beach bar at the tip of De Palm Pier on busy Palm Beach is hopping and bopping with visitors and locals alike. Paint-spattered wooden tables and chairs on a plank floor under a massive palapa draw barefoot beachcombers for frozen cocktails, cold beer, and casual fare where live music is king. The revelry starts as early as happy hour, and continues well into the evening. Karaoke night, salsa night, and even a crazy fish night on Monday: there's always something wild and fun going on there. It's also an optimal spot to catch a magical sunset over the waves. There's free Wi-Fi, too. ⊠ *De Palm Pier, J. E. Irausquin Blvd. 79, Palm Beach* ☎ *297/586–2233* ⊕ *www.bugaloe.com.*

CLOSE UP

Brewing Up Something Special

Order a "Balashi cocktail" in Aruba only if you want to receive a glass of water. That's because the water purification plant is in Balashi. And don't be afraid to drink the water: it's safe and delicious and made from desalinated seawater. But since the advent of the beer called Balashi—the only beer in the world made from desalinated seawater—you might confuse a barkeep if you order just a "Balashi." The brewery has regularly scheduled tours should you want to see how it's made, and they also have a great beer garden and lunch spot. They are making a second type of beer there now: Balashi Chill. It's best enjoyed with a wedge of lime in the neck like many Mexican beers. Simply order a "Chill," and most barkeeps on the island will understand.

Café Rembrandt. Great schnitzels, hearty fare, and really low prices on cold imported beer and drinks bring Dutch expats in droves, and then everyone stays longer for the great camaraderie, twice-nightly happy hours, and the warm and friendly staff. There's occasional live music, and dancing usually on weekends. ⊠ *South Beach Centre, Palm Beach* ☎ *297/586–4747* ⊕ *www.facebook.com/cafe rembrandt* ⊗ *Closed Mon.*

★ Fodor'sChoice **Gusto.** Definitely Aruba's most cosmopolitan, high-octane dance club where master bartenders show off their skills while serving fabulous cocktails with excellent flair. Plenty of pretty people, the island's hottest DJ's, and a dazzling light show keep the dancing going nonstop. Late-night happy hour is 9–11. All kinds of special events and theme nights add to Gusto's allure as a highly popular party spot. ⊠ *J. E. Irausquin Blvd. 348-A, Palm Beach* ⊗ *Closed Mon.*

Local Store. Contrary to its name, it's not a store but a bar, and a very local one at that. Live local bands, lots of resident partiers, and a laid-back, down-to-earth atmosphere make this the place to kick back and have fun, especially on weekends. Good prices on drinks, local beer, craft beers, and local Aruban snacks like *funchi* fries all add to the allure. ⊠ *Palm Beach 13A, Noord* ☎ *297/586–1414* ⊕ *www. localstorearuba.com* ⊗ *Sun.–Thurs. 11 am–midnight, Fri. and Sat. 11 am–2 am.*

Cool Concoctions

Aruba's skilled staff are, for the most part, far more than barkeeps; many are master mixologists who have trained in well-accredited institutions both on the island and abroad—they also often compete in international competitions. So before ordering a tried-and-true tropical favorite like a piña colada or the Island's best-known drink, the Aruba Ariba, bring a smile to their face by asking them to make you one of their original concoctions or a signature cocktail from the establishment's own bar menu. The taste and creativity is sure to bring a smile to your face, too, and many of the specials are handcrafted with home-grown ingredients and artisanal liquors. And even if it's not the Christmas season, do seek out a sample of *ponche crema*— Aruba's extremely liquor-laden and beautifully spiced eggnog that's available year-round (and in take-home bottles). Also seek out *coecoei*, a unique Aruban liqueur that tastes like anisette but is thicker and ruby red in color. It colors many island drinks instead of grenadine and is also good by itself on the rocks.

★ Fodor'sChoice **MooMba Beach Bar.** As the central party spot on the busiest part of Palm Beach, this open-air bar is famous for its Sunday night blowouts with big crowds of locals gathering to dance in the sand to live bands or DJ's. The barkeeps are flair and mixology masters, and happy hours are also very hot. Its sister dining establishment is a wonderful surfside spot for breakfast, lunch, and dinner. ⊠ *Between Holiday Inn and Marriott Surf Club, J. E. Irausquin Blvd. 230, Palm Beach* 🕾 *297/586–5365* ⊕ *www.moombabeach.com.*

Palms Beach Bar. A casual alfresco surfside lounge, Palms Beach Bar is an inviting spot to watch the sunset over a signature cocktail or to catch sporting events on their large-screen TVs. It's a more intimate place, perfect for taking in the tropical night in between barhopping at busier hot spots. Lunch and dinner menus are also available. ⊠ *Hyatt Regency Aruba Beach Resort & Casino, J. E. Irausquin Blvd. 85, Palm Beach* 🕾 *297/586–1234* ⊕ *aruba.hyatt.com.*

Señor Frog's. True to most of its locations, this chain bar is a hot spot that pulls in a wild crowd of tourists. The music is loud, and the crowd is pumped up by the animated staff and such alcoholic favorites as the "yard of beer" (you can also buy a "yard" of margaritas). Either way, you can take the glass home with you. This is definitely a popular stop

for younger partiers. ✉ *J. E. Irausquin Blvd., Palm Beach* ☎ *297/569–9006* ⊕ *www.senorfrogs.com.*

Sopranos Piano Bar. With a theme loosely based on the famous HBO series, Sopranos has a fun atmosphere, and live piano nightly encourages the crowd to join in a sing-along. Top-notch barkeeps shake up a big list of creative cocktails, including their famous signature drink, the Bikini Martini. An extensive wine list (for a piano bar) and a cigar lounge add to its allure. Doors open at 5 pm, and live music begins at 8 pm. Sometimes there are DJs late on weekends. ✉ *Arawak Garden Mall, L. G. Smith Blvd. 177, Palm Beach* ☎ *297/586-8622* ⊕ *www.sopranospianobar.com.*

A MYRIAD OF MUSIC FESTIVALS

Aruba has gone wild for live musical events in the past few years, and they run the gamut from blues and jazz to techno and electronic to old-fashioned folkloric like the New Year's Dande competition and Carnival march music contests. Visit ⊕ *www.aruba.com* and search events for all the listings.

PERFORMING ARTS

Aruba has a handful of not-quite-famous but very talented stars. Over the years, several local artists, including composer Julio Renado Euson, choreographer Wilma Kuiperi, sculptor Ciro Abath, and visual artist Elvis Lopez, have gained international renown. Further, many Aruban musicians play more than one type of music (classical, jazz, soca, salsa, reggae, calypso, rap, pop), and many compose as well as perform. Edjean Semeleer has followed in the footsteps of his mentor Padu Lampe—the composer of the island's national anthem and a beloved local star—to become one of the island's best-loved entertainers. His performances pack Aruba's biggest halls, especially his annual Christmas concert. He sings in many languages, and though he's young, his style is "old-school crooner"—Aruba's answer to Michael Bublé.

Cas Di Cultura. The National Theater of Aruba, the island's cultural center, hosts art exhibits, folkloric shows, dance performances, and concerts throughout the year. ✉ *Vondellaan 2, Oranjestad* ☎ *297/582–1010* ⊕ *www.casdicultura.aw.*

Art in Aruba

Aruba's art scene is eclectic and evolving, with lots of multimedia artists as well as traditional painters who work in oils, like Elvis Tromp. You'll see lots of interesting media scattered around the island in outdoor art as well, like the mirrored ceramic sculptures at the airport art garden. The boardwalks of the new Linear Park will be prime real estate for the island's creative types to showcase their works.

One local talent has created a new kind of art hybrid recently. Her name is Elisa Lejuez Peters, and she is fast becoming one of Aruba's best-known artists. Her signature works of "neo-pop" art, inspired by her studies in fashion and textiles, have become wearable with the creation of her new line of avant-garde clothing. Her artwork has also been shown in New York, and no doubt you'll recognize her signature style gracing the walls of many major hotels, restaurants, and public buildings.

Another avant-garde Aruban artist is sculptor Gilbert Senchi, whose massive iron installations and offbeat works have been commissioned by the government to enhance public spaces and to give as gifts to the Dutch royal family. Then there is up-and-coming young artist Armando Goedgedrag, a multimedia specialist whose talent as a painter is also becoming well known. He's an avid surfer, and his photos and paintings of Aruba's wildest waves are making waves of their own.

As far as where you can go to see or purchase art, Aruba has a few small galleries, but the art scene really consists more of a revolving series of community exhibitions and shows, or classes in artists' residences like Ciro and Marian Abath's home workshop, where they invite guests to come and learn to work in glass, ceramic, and bronze.

The pop-up art show series in downtown Oranjestad turns an empty street into a temporary outdoor gallery, but there is one new spot where you can always see Aruban art: a permanent collection at UNOCA—Aruba's first national gallery—is always on display. They have rotating exhibits of local and international artists as well. You will find the UNOCA building in downtown Oranjestad a few blocks from Cas di Cultura, which also has occasional art shows.

6

Carnival

CLOSE UP

Aruba's biggest bash incorporates local traditions with those of Venezuela, Brazil, Holland, and North America. Trinidadians who came to work at the oil refinery in the 1940s introduced Carnival to the island, so it's only fitting that the new Carnival Village, Workshop and Museum was built in San Nicolas, where it all began. Though the town they call Sunrise City has always been the location for Carnival's Jouvert Morning Jump-Up (also called the Pajama Party, since it begins at 4 am and many people come straight from bed), most of the festivities have been held in Oranjestad over the years. Now the monthlong celebration swings more between the two towns with pageants, parades, musical competitions, ceremonies, and gala concerts in both. But the Grand Parade held on the Sunday before Ash Wednesday still takes over all of downtown Oranjestad with thousands dancing in the streets and viewing the floats, costumes, and bands. All events end on Shrove Tuesday: at midnight an effigy of King Momo (traditionally depicted as a fat man) is burned, indicating the end of joy and the beginning of Lenten penitence. You can get a taste of the carnival spirit every Thursday night in San Nicolas with the Carubbian Festival held year-round.

ART GALLERIES

Gasparito Restaurant & Art Gallery. A permanent exhibition by a variety of Aruban artists is featured here, ranging from colorful landscapes to more abstract offerings. ⊠ *Gasparito 3, Noord* ☎ 297/586–7044.

Insight Art Studio. Owner Alida Martinez, a Venezuelan-born artist, likes more avant-garde displays, so don't expect to find the usual paintings of pastel-color skies here. Inventive works by local and international artists are featured. Martinez's own mixed-media creations juxtapose erotic and religious themes. The space, which includes a studio, is a magnet for the island's art community. Viewing is by appointment only. ⊠ *Paradera Park 215, Paradera* ☎ 297/582–5882.

FESTIVALS

Finally, the island's many festivals showcase arts and culture. To find out what's going on, check out the local English-language newspapers or look for events online at ⊕ *www.aruba.com.*

ANNUAL EVENTS

Caribbean Sea Jazz Festival. The music begins at intimate venues around the island and leads up to a big two-day jazz, soul, and Latin music festival held at the Renaissance Marketplace, usually in the third week of September. Big-name bands draw big crowds to the harbor, and the outdoor party continues long into the night all around Oranjestad with makeshift food stands and temporary bars. There is also a big on-site art event during the fest. ✉ *Renaissance Marketplace, Oranjestad* ⊕ *www.caribbeanseajazz.com.*

Carubbian Festival. Every Thursday night in San Nicolas, the main streets of Aruba's old refinery town that locals called "Sunrise City" come to life in a spectacular fashion with a minicarnival called the Carubbian Festival. It's a culture and heritage extravaganza featuring live music concerts, dancing shows, and even a big colorful parade finale where visitors are encouraged to fully participate. There are also arts-and-crafts stalls and food-and-drink kiosks that include local specialties set up for the occasion. There are activities planned for children as well. The festival runs 6–10 pm. ■TIP→ You are best to take a hotel bus package as the roads at night are not lighted, and navigation can be challenging. ✉ *Main St., San Nicolas* 🎟 *Free.*

The Dande Festival. Aruba's New Year traditions begin with a big bang before the big day, when Arubans light *pagaras* (strings of hundreds of firecrackers) all over the island to celebrate a good year and chase out bad vibes. New Year's Eve sees the traditional islandwide fireworks, but they also usher in the New Year with Dande music. It used to be a "stroll" with groups of musicians going from house to house singing good-luck greetings right after midnight, but now it has become a bona-fide organized festival held with big groups competing for prizes on December 27. *Dande* comes from the Papiamento word *dandara,* which means "to have a good time." ⊕ *www.aruba.com/things-to-do/dande-festival.*

Dera Gai (St. John's Day). The annual harvest feast and *dera gai* ("burying of the rooster") tradition is celebrated June 24, the feast of St. John the Baptist. Festive songs, bright yellow-and-red costumes, and traditional dances mark this holiday, which dates to 1862. Today, the live rooster—which symbolizes a successful harvest—has been replaced by a plastic one. You will also notice smoke all around the island from the ceremonial bonfires traditionally lighted that day. ⊕ *www.aruba.com/things-to-do/dera-gai-st-johns-day.*

Divi Aruba International Beach Tennis Tournament. Aruba has become the beach-tennis capital of the Caribbean, with its own leagues and global competitors. Each year Divi Aruba hosts an international tournament on Eagle Beach in conjunction with the International Tennis Federation, with big cash incentives for the winners, such as $25,000 in prize money. Some 800 players from all over the globe converge on the island for a weeklong event in September that includes parties, live music, food courts, and all kinds of special events. Many activity operators also offer beach-tennis lessons for visitors on a regular basis. ⊠ *Eagle Beach* ⊕ *www.divibeachtennisaruba.com.*

Hi-Winds Pro Am Windsurfing Competition. Windsurfers of all skill levels from more than 30 different countries converge in June and July to compete off the beaches at Fisherman's Huts at Hadikurari. Celebrating its 30th year in 2016, this has become the biggest windsurfing and kiteboarding event of the Caribbean, complete with a massive beach celebration, throngs of fans, and lots of music with a party that lasts for days. Mountain-bike races have been added, and the world's best kiteboarders compete here too. ⊠ *Fisherman's Huts Beach* ⊕ *www.hiwindsaruba.com.*

National Anthem & Flag Day. On March 18, an official holiday, you can stop by Plaza Betico Croes in Oranjestad for folkloric presentations and other traditional festivities. Everyone has flags and is out in the streets; be prepared for just about every business to be closed that day for the celebrations. There are also special sporting events. ⊕ *www.aruba.com/things-to-do/national-anthem-and-flag-day.*

★ Fodor'sChoice **Soul Beach Festival.** Going into its 16th year in 2016, this big festival is becoming the island's top musical event. Held over Memorial Day weekend in May, it attracts big-name artists and huge crowds with concerts rotating locations from Palm Beach to downtown Oranjestad all the way to San Nicolas. There are also comedy shows, the new Soul Beach Fitness Challenge, and parties galore islandwide. ⊠ *Palm Beach.*

CASINOS

AMONG THE BIGGEST DRAWS in Aruba are the island's elaborate, pulsating casinos. Aruba offers up gambling venues closer in spirit and form to Las Vegas than any other island in the Caribbean. Perhaps it's the predominantly American crowd, but the casinos remain busy and popular, and almost every big resort has one. Although people don't dress as elegantly as they did in years gone by, most of the casinos still expect a somewhat more put-together look (in the evening, at least) than a T-shirt and flip-flops.

There was a time when women dressed in evening gowns and men donned suits for a chic, glamorous night in Aruba's casinos. In the mid-'80s, however, the Alhambra Casino opened, touting its philosophy of "barefoot elegance." Suddenly shorts and T-shirts became acceptable attire. The relaxed dress code made gaming seem an affordable pastime rather than a luxury.

Aruba's casinos now attract high rollers, low-stakes bettors, and nongamblers alike. Games include slot machines and blackjack (both beloved by North Americans), baccarat (preferred by South Americans), craps, roulette—even betting on sports events. Theaters, restaurants, bars, and cigar shops have added another dimension to the casinos. Now you can go out for dinner, take in a show, sip after-dinner drinks, and play blackjack all under one roof. In between games, you can get to know other patrons and swap tips and tales. The many local entertainers who rotate among the casinos add to the excitement.

GAMBLING PRIMER

For a short-form handbook on the rules, the odds, and the strategies for the most popular casino games—or for help deciding on the kind of action that suits your style—read on.

THE GOOD BETS

The first part of any viable casino strategy is to risk the most money on wagers that present the lowest edge for the house. Blackjack, craps, video poker, and baccarat are the most advantageous to the bettor in this regard. The two types of bets at baccarat have a house advantage of a little more than 1%. The basic line bets at craps, if backed up with full odds, can be as low as 0.5%. Blackjack and video poker, at times, have a house edge that's less than 1%

The vibrant casino at the Ritz Carlton

(nearly a 50–50 proposition), and with bettor diligence can actually present a slight long-term advantage.

How can a casino possibly provide you with a potentially positive expectation at some of its games? First, because a vast number of gamblers make bad bets (at games with a house advantage of 5%–35%, like roulette, keno, and slots) day in and day out. Second, because the casino knows that very few people are aware of the opportunities to beat the odds. Third, because it takes skill—requiring study and practice—to be in a position to exploit these opportunities. However, a mere hour or two spent learning strategies for the beatable games will put you light-years ahead of the vast majority of visitors who contribute to the gambling industry's 12%–15% average profit margin.

THE GAMES

BACCARAT

The most "glamorous" game in the casino, baccarat is a version of *chemin de fer,* which is popular in European gambling halls. It's a favorite with high rollers because thousands of dollars are often staked on one hand. The Italian word *baccara* means "zero." This refers to the point value of 10s and picture cards. The game is run by four pit personnel. Two dealers sit side by side at the middle of the table. They handle the winning and losing bets and keep track of each player's "commission". The caller stands in the middle of the other side of the table and dictates the action. The "ladderman" supervises the game and acts as final judge if any disputes arise.

HOW TO PLAY

Baccarat is played with eight decks of cards dealt from a large "shoe" (or cardholder). Each player is offered a turn at handling the shoe and dealing the cards. Two two-card hands are dealt facedown: the "player" and the "bank" hands. The player who deals the cards is called the banker, although the house banks both hands. The players bet on which hand—player or banker—will come closest to adding up to 9 (a "natural"). Ace through 9 retain face value, and 10s and picture cards are worth zero. If you have a hand adding up to more than 10, the number 10 is subtracted from the total. For example, if one hand contains a 10 and a 4, the hand adds up to 4. If the other holds an ace and a 6, it adds up to 7. If a hand has a 7 and a 9, it adds up to 6.

Depending on the two hands, the caller either declares a winner and loser (if either hand actually adds up to 8 or 9) or calls for another card for the player hand (if it totals 1, 2, 3, 4, 5, or 10). The bank hand then either stands pat or draws a card, determined by a complex series of rules depending on what the player's total is and dictated by the caller. When one or the other hand is declared a winner, the dealers go into action to pay off the winning wagers, collect the losing wagers, and add up the commission (usually 5%) that the house collects on the bank hand. Both bets have a house advantage of slightly more than 1%.

The player-dealer (or banker) holds the shoe as long as the bank hand wins. When the player hand wins, the shoe moves counterclockwise around the table. Players can refuse the shoe and pass it to the next player. Because the caller dictates the action, player responsibilities are minimal. It's not necessary to know the card-drawing rules, even if you're the banker.

BACCARAT STRATEGY

To bet, you only have to place your money in the bank, player, or tie box on the layout, which appears directly in front of where you sit. If you're betting that the bank hand will win, you put your chips in the bank box; bets for the player hand go in the player box. (Only real suckers bet on the tie.) Most players bet on the bank hand when they deal, since they "represent" the bank and to do otherwise would seem as if they were betting "against" themselves. This isn't really true, but it seems that way. Playing baccarat is a simple matter of guessing whether the player or banker hand will come closest to 9 and deciding how much to bet on the outcome.

BLACKJACK

HOW TO PLAY

You play blackjack against a dealer, and whichever of you comes closest to a card total of 21 wins. Number cards are worth their face value, picture cards are worth 10, and aces are worth either 1 or 11. (Hands with aces are known as "soft" hands. Always count the ace first as an 11. If you also have a 10, your total will be 21, not 11.) If the dealer has a 17 and you have a 16, you lose. If you have an 18 against a dealer's 17, you win (even money). If both you and the dealer have a 17, it's a tie (or "push") and no money changes hands. If you go over a total of 21 (or "bust"), you lose, even if the dealer also busts later in the hand. If your first two cards add up to 21 (a "natural"), you're paid 3 to 2. However, if the dealer also has a natural, it's a push. A natural beats a total of 21 achieved with more than two cards.

You're dealt two cards, either facedown or faceup, depending on the custom of the casino. The dealer also gives herself two cards, one facedown and one faceup (except in double-exposure blackjack, where both the dealer's cards are visible). Depending on your first two cards and the dealer's up card, you can **stand,** or refuse to take another card. You can **hit,** or take as many cards as you need until you stand or bust. You can **double down,** or double your bet and take one card. You can **split** a like pair: if you're dealt two 8s, for example, you can double your bet and play the 8s as if they're two hands. You can **buy insurance** if the dealer is showing an ace. Here you're wagering half your initial bet that the dealer *does* have a natural. If so, you lose your initial bet but are paid 2 to 1 on the insurance (which means the whole thing is a push). You can **surrender** half your initial bet if you're holding a bad hand (known as a "stiff") such as a 15 or 16 against a high-up card such as a 9 or 10.

BLACKJACK STRATEGY

Many people devote a great deal of time to learning complicated statistical schemes. However, if you don't have the time, energy, or inclination to get that seriously involved, the following basic strategies should allow you to play the game with a modicum of skill and a paucity of humiliation:

When your hand totals 12, 13, 14, 15, or 16, and the dealer shows a 2, 3, 4, 5, or 6, you should stand. *Exception:* If your hand totals 12, and the dealer shows a 2 or 3, you should hit.

When your hand totals 12, 13, 14, 15, or 16, and the dealer shows a 7, 8, 9, 10, or ace, always hit.

When you hold 17, 18, 19, or 20, always stand.

When you hold a 10 or 11 and the dealer shows a 2, 3, 4, 5, 6, 7, 8, or 9, always double down.

When you hold a pair of aces or a pair of 8s, always split.

Never buy insurance.

CRAPS

Craps is a fast-paced, action-packed dice game that can require up to four pit personnel to run. Two dealers handle the bets made on either side of the layout. A "stickman" wields the long wooden stick, curved at one end, which is used to move the dice around the table. The stickman also calls the number that's rolled and books the proposition bets made in the middle of the layout. The "boxman" sits between the two dealers, overseeing the game and settling any disputes.

HOW TO PLAY

Stand at the table wherever you can find an open space. You can start betting casino chips immediately, but you have to wait your turn to be the shooter. The dice are passed clockwise around the table (the stickman will give you the dice at the appropriate time). It's important, when you're the shooter, to roll the dice hard enough so they bounce off the end wall of the table. This shows that you're not trying to control the dice with a "soft roll."

Playing craps is fairly straightforward; it's the betting that's complicated. The basic concepts are as follows: if the first time the shooter rolls the dice (called the "come-out roll") he or she turns up a 7 or 11, that's called a "natural"—an automatic win. If a 2, 3, or 12 comes up on the first throw, that's termed "craps"—an automatic lose. Each of the numbers 4, 5, 6, 8, 9, or 10 on a first roll is known as a "point": the shooter keeps rolling the dice until the point comes up again. If a 7 turns up before the point does, that's

DID YOU KNOW?

Aruba offers the closest thing in the Caribbean to Las Vegas–style casino action, with some casinos in large hotels open 24 hours a day; the legal age for gambling is 18.

another loser. When either the point or a losing 7 is rolled, this is known as a "decision," which happens on average every 3.3 rolls.

CRAPS STRATEGY

"Winning" and "losing" rolls of the dice are entirely relative in this game, because there are two ways you can bet at craps: "for" the shooter or "against" the shooter. Betting for means that the shooter will "make his point" (win). Betting against means that the shooter will "seven out" (lose). Either way, you're actually betting against the house, which books all wagers. If you're betting "for" on the come-out, you place your chips on the layout's "pass line." If a 7 or 11 is rolled, you win even money. If a 2, 3, or 12 (craps) is rolled, you lose your bet. If you're betting "against" on the come-out, you place your chips in the "don't pass bar." A 7 or 11 loses; a 2, 3, or 12 wins. A shooter can bet for or against himself, or against other players.

There are also roughly two dozen wagers you can make on any single specific roll of the dice. Craps strategy books can give you the details on come/don't come, odds, place, buy, big six, field, and proposition bets.

ROULETTE

Roulette is a casino game that uses a perfectly balanced wheel with 38 numbers (0, 00, and 1 through 36), a small white ball, a large layout with 11 different betting options, and special "wheel chips." The layout organizes 11 different bets into 6 "inside bets" (the single numbers, or those closest to the dealer) and 5 "outside bets" (the grouped bets, or those closest to the players).

The dealer spins the wheel clockwise and the ball counterclockwise. When the ball slows, the dealer announces, "No more bets." The ball drops from the "back track" to the "bottom track," caroming off built-in brass barriers and bouncing in and out of the different cups in the wheel before settling into the cup of the winning number. Then the dealer places a marker on the number and scoops all the losing chips into her corner. Depending on how crowded the game is, the casino can count on roughly 50 spins of the wheel per hour.

HOW TO PLAY

To buy in, place your cash on the layout near the wheel. Inform the dealer of the denomination of the individual unit you intend to play. Know the table limits (displayed on a sign in the dealer area). Don't ask for a 25¢ denomination if the minimum is $1. The dealer gives you a stack of wheel chips of a color that's different from those of all the other players and places a chip marker atop one of your wheel chips on the rim of the wheel to identify its denomination. Note that you must cash in your wheel chips at the roulette table before you leave the game. Only the dealer can verify how much they're worth.

ROULETTE STRATEGY

With **inside bets,** you can lay any number of chips (depending on the table limits) on a single number, 1 through 36 or 0 or 00. If the number hits, your payoff is 35 to 1, for a return of $36. You could, conceivably, place a $1 chip on all 38 numbers, but the return of $36 would leave you $2 short, which divides out to 5.26%, the house advantage. If you place a chip on the line between two numbers and one of those numbers hits, you're paid 17 to 1 for a return of $18 (again, $2 short of the true odds). Betting on three numbers returns 11 to 1, four numbers returns 8 to 1, five numbers pays 6 to 1 (this is the worst bet at roulette, with a 7.89% disadvantage), and six numbers pays 5 to 1.

To place an **outside bet,** lay a chip on one of three "columns" at the lower end of the layout next to numbers 34, 35, and 36. This pays 2 to 1. A bet placed in the first 12, second 12, or third 12 boxes also pays 2 to 1. A bet on red or black, odd or even, and 1 through 18 or 19 through 36 pays off at even money, 1 to 1. If you think you can bet on red *and* black, or odd *and* even, in order to play roulette and drink for free all night, think again. The green 0 or 00, which fall outside these two basic categories, will come up on average once every 19 spins of the wheel.

SLOT MACHINES
HOW TO PLAY

Playing slots is basically the same as it's always been. But the look and feel of the games has changed dramatically in the last several years. Machines that used to dispense a noisy waterfall of coins have all but given way to new generations of machines that pay out wins with printed coded tickets instead of coins. If you are a historian, or sentimental, you can still find a few coin-dispensing relics, but in the larger casinos they've almost all been replaced by the new ticketing payout system. These tickets can be inserted into other slot machines like cash, or can be redeemed at the cage or at ATM-like machines that dispense cash right on the casino floor. Nowadays many of the games are all-digital, with touch screens, and play like video games. But the underlying concept is still the same: after you start the game, you're looking for the reels—real or virtual—to match a winning pattern of shapes.

SLOT-MACHINE STRATEGY

The house advantage on slots varies from machine to machine, between 3% and 25%. Casinos that advertise a 97% payback are telling you that at least one of their slot machines has a house advantage of 3%. Which one? There's really no way of knowing. Generally, $1 machines pay back at a higher percentage than 25¢ or 5¢ machines. On the other hand, machines with smaller jackpots pay back more money more frequently, meaning that you'll be playing with more of your winnings.

One of the all-time great myths about slot machines is that they're "due" for a jackpot. Slots, like roulette, craps, keno, and Big Six, are subject to the Law of Independent Trials, which means the odds are permanently and unalterably fixed. If the odds of lining up three sevens on a 25¢ slot machine have been set by the casino at 1 in 10,000, then those odds remain 1 in 10,000 whether the three 7s have been hit three times in a row or not hit for 90,000 plays. Don't waste a lot of time playing a machine that you suspect is "ready," and don't think if someone hits a jackpot on a particular machine only minutes after you've finished playing on it that it was "yours."

VIDEO POKER

This section deals only with straight-draw video poker.

Like blackjack, video poker is a game of strategy and skill, and at select times on select machines the player actually holds the advantage, however slight, over the house. Unlike with slot machines, you can determine the exact edge of video-poker machines. Like slots, however, video-poker machines are often tied into a progressive meter; when the jackpot total reaches high enough, you can beat the casino at its own game. The variety of video-poker machines is growing steadily. All are played in similar fashion, but the strategies are different.

HOW TO PLAY

The schedule for the payback on winning hands is posted on the machine, usually above the screen. It lists the returns for a high pair (generally jacks or better), two pair, three

A Roulette table at the Marriott's Stellaris Casino

of a kind, a flush, full house, straight flush, four of a kind, and royal flush, depending on the number of coins played—usually 1, 2, 3, 4, or 5. Look for machines that pay with a single coin played: 1 coin for "jacks or better" (meaning a pair of jacks, queens, kings, or aces; any other pair is a stiff), 2 coins for two pairs, 3 for three of a kind, 6 for a flush, 9 for a full house, 50 for a straight flush, 100 for four of a kind, and 250 for a royal flush. This is known as a 9/6 machine—one that gives a nine-coin payback for a full house and a six-coin payback for a flush with one coin played. Other machines are known as 8/5 (eight for a full house, five for a flush), 7/5, and 6/5.

You want a 9/6 machine because it gives you the best odds: the return from a standard 9/6 straight-draw machine is 99.5%; you give up half a percent to the house. An 8/5 machine returns 97.3%. On 6/5 machines, the figure drops to 95.1%, slightly less than roulette. Machines with varying paybacks are scattered throughout the casinos. In some you'll see an 8/5 machine right next to a 9/6, and someone will be blithely playing the 8/5 machine.

As with slot machines, it's best to play the maximum number of coins to qualify for the jackpot. You insert five coins into the slot and press the "deal" button. Five cards appear on the screen—say, 5, jack, queen, 5, 9. To hold the pair of 5s, you press the hold buttons under the first and fourth cards. The word "hold" appears underneath the two 5s.

You then press the "draw" button (often the same button as "deal") and three new cards appear on the screen—say, 10, jack, 5. You have three 5s. With five coins bet, the machine will give you 15 credits. Now you can press the "max bet" button: five units will be removed from your credits, and five new cards will appear on the screen. You repeat the hold-and-draw process; if you hit a winning hand, the proper payback will be added to your credits.

VIDEO-POKER STRATEGY

Like blackjack, video poker has a basic strategy that's been formulated by the computer simulation of hundreds of millions of hands. The most effective way to learn it is with a video-poker computer program that deals the cards on your screen, then tutors you in how to play each hand properly. If you don't want to devote that much time to the study of video poker, memorizing these six rules will help you make the right decision for more than half the hands you'll be dealt:

1. If you're dealt a completely "stiff" hand (no like cards and no picture cards), draw five new cards.

2. If you're dealt a hand with no like cards but with one jack, queen, king, or ace, always hold on to the picture card; if you're dealt two different picture cards, hold both. But if you're dealt three different picture cards, hold only two (the two of the same suit, if that's an option).

3. If you're dealt a pair, hold it—no matter the face value.

4. Never hold a picture card with a pair of 2s through 10s.

5. Never draw two cards to try for a straight or a flush.

6. Never draw one card to try for an inside straight.

THE CASINOS

Most casinos are found in hotels; all are along Palm Beach or Eagle Beach or in downtown Oranjestad. Although the minimum age to enter is 18, some venues are relaxed about this rule. By day, "barefoot elegance" is the norm in all casinos, although many establishments have a shirt-and-shoes requirement. Evening dress is expected to be more polished, though still casual. In high season the casinos are open from just before noon to the wee hours; in low season (May–November) they may not start dealing until late afternoon.

If you plan to play large sums of money, check in with the casino upon arrival so that you can be rewarded for your business. Most hotels offer gambling goodies—complimentary meals at local restaurants, chauffeured tours, and, in the cases of big spenders, high-roller suites. Even small-scale gamblers may be entitled to coupons for meals and discounted rooms.

ORANJESTAD AND ENVIRONS

Alhambra Casino. Recently refurbished and refreshed as part of the new Alhambra Mall reconstruction, this is a lively popular casino with a big selection of modern slots, blackjack, craps, poker, roulette and more. Be sure to join their Player's Club—it's free and offers free slot credits, and you earn points with your card as well. Their new restaurant called The Cove serves light meals and drinks, and you'll also receive free drinks on the floor when playing the games. Special theme nights and promotions are offered all week, and Saturday afternoon they have Super Bingo. It is owned by the Divi family of resorts. ⊠ *L. G. Smith Blvd. 47, Oranjestad* ☎ *297/583–5000* ⊕ *www.casino alhambra.com.*

Crystal Casino. Adorned with Austrian crystal chandeliers and gold-leaf columns, the Renaissance Aruba's glittering casino evokes Monaco's grand establishments. The Salon Privé offers serious gamblers a private room for baccarat, roulette, and high-stakes blackjack. This casino is popular among cruise-ship passengers, who stroll over from the port to watch and play in slot tournaments and to bet on sporting events. Luxury car giveaways are also a big draw there. It's open daily 11 am–6 am. ⊠ *Renaissance Aruba Resort & Casino, L. G. Smith Blvd. 82, Oranjestad* ☎ *297/583–6000.*

★ Fodor's Choice **Seaport Casino.** A super-lively and fun casino right on the waterfront and across the street from the lively Renaissance Marketplace, this place has more than 300 modern slots as well as 6 blackjack tables, Caribbean Stud, roulette, regular poker, and Texas Hold 'Em. Sister to Crystal Casino close by, they give away luxury cars and offer $5 free-play slot cards. They also have state-of-the-art race and sports book operations. ⊠ *L. G. Smith Blvd. 9, Oranjestad* ☎ *297/583–6000.*

PALM BEACH AND NOORD

Aura Casino. The Occidental Grand Aruba's Aura Casino never sleeps as long as there are players in the house. Craps, poker, blackjack, roulette, hot slots, and bingo—it's got it all. Las Vegas–style shows and dancing at Sound add to the action. Slots start at noon, and tables and machines open at 5 pm. ⊠ *Occidental Grand Aruba, J. E. Irausquin Blvd. 83, Palm Beach* ☎ *297/586–9039* ⊕ *www.occidentalhotels.com.*

Casino at the Ritz-Carlton Aruba. A big, brand-new, and very "ritzy" casino just off the lobby of the Ritz-Carlton Aruba offers many traditional table games like blackjack, craps, roulette, Caribbean Stud poker, baccarat, and Texas Hold 'Em, as well as more than 300 modern slots: spinning reels, video reels, and video games with jackpots available 24/7. Tables run 6 pm–3 am. They also have two sports-betting kiosks and offer "luxury" bingo several times a week. Points accumulated from their VIP casino-club card can be used toward hotel extras like dining, spa treatments, and room nights. ⊠ *L. G. Smith Blvd. 107, Noord* ☎ *297/527–2222* ⊕ *www.ritzcarlton.com/en/Properties/ Aruba/Casino/Default.htm.*

The Casino at the Radisson Aruba Resort. Famous for its starry indoor skies, this casino is smaller than some, but very popular with locals as well as visitors. With typical slots, gaming tables, and good poker action, a nice touch is their new Hora Loca crazy hour, when the first 50 people on slots at 8 pm Wednesday get $10 free play. They also have a loyalty program. Bingo weekends and special theme nights occasionally draw players, and they are open until 4 am seven days a week. ⊠ *J. E. Irausquin Blvd. 81, Palm Beach* ☎ *297/526–6930* ⊕ *www.facebook.com/thecasinoradisson* ⊗ *Daily noon–4 am.*

Cool Casino. At this very tiny casino in the Riu Palace, it seems gambling is more of an afterthought than the bar. It does have blackjack and baccarat tables, some slots, and roulette, though. Live music adds to the barlike atmosphere. ⊠ *Riu Palace, J. E. Irausquin Blvd. 79, Palm Beach* ☎ *297/586–3900* ⊕ *www.coolcasinoaruba.com/new-site.*

Excelsior Casino. Located in the Holiday Inn Aruba, this is one of the oldest casinos on the island and features the largest poker room with limits as low as $2–$4 to $50–$100 no limit. A good selection of standard slots and daily bingo, blackjack, craps, and roulette tables round out the offer-

Good-Luck Charms

Arubans take myths and superstitions very seriously. They flinch if a black butterfly flits into their home, because this symbolizes death. And on New Year's Eve they toss the first sips of whiskey, rum, or champagne from the first bottle that's opened in the New Year out the door of their house to show respect to those who have died and to wish luck on others. It's no surprise, then, that good-luck charms are part of Aruba's casino culture as well.

The island's most common good-luck charm is the *djucu*

(pronounced *joo*-koo), a brown-and-black stone that comes from the sea and becomes hot when rubbed. It's often called the "lucky nut." Many people have them put in gold settings—with their initials engraved in the metal—and wear them around their necks on a chain with other charms such as an anchor or a cross. Another item that's thought to bring good luck is a small bag of sand. The older generation of women might wear them tucked discreetly into their bras.

ings. Slots open early at 9 am, tables at noon. ⊠ *Holiday Inn Resort Aruba, J. E. Irausquin Blvd. 230, Palm Beach* ☎ *297/586–7777, 297/586–3600* ⊕ *www.excelsiorcasino. com.*

Hyatt Regency Casino. Ablaze with neon, with a Carnival-in-Rio theme, the most popular games here are slots, blackjack, craps, and baccarat. In the heart of the main tourist strip in one of the nicest hotels along Palm Beach, this gambling emporium is also known for its live music Thursday–Sunday and lively party atmosphere. Don't forget to ask for your $10 free-play card. It's open until 4 am. ⊠ *Hyatt Regency Aruba Beach Resort & Casino, J. E. Irausquin Blvd. 85, Palm Beach* ☎ *297/586–1234* ⊕ *www. aruba.hyatt.com.*

★ Fodor's Choice **Stellaris Casino.** This is the largest casino on the island and boasts 500 modern interactive slots and 28 tables with games like craps, roulette, poker, and blackjack. They also have a state-of-the-art race and sports betting operation. Don't forget to join their VIP Club, where you can earn points, comps, and prizes. Free cocktails for gamers, and there are many special theme and entertainment nights. ⊠ *Aruba Marriott Resort, L. G. Smith Blvd. 101, Palm Beach* ☎ *297/520–6428.*

7

Trop Club & Casino. Newly refreshed and completely reno-
vated in 2015, the new Trop Club & Casino is slot city,
and they guarantee they'll offer a 30% payout increase.
Video slots, progressive slots, and reel slot titles all offer
hassle-free gaming via ticket-in, ticket-out technology. Table
games include roulette, three-card poker, Let It Ride, and
blackjack. The table-game atmosphere is pretty hot, too.
And the new Double Down Sports Bar & Grill is worth
a visit on its own. ⊠ *Tropicana Aruba Resort & Casino,
J. E. Irausquin Blvd. 248, Eagle Beach* ☎ *297/587–9000*
⊕ *www.troparuba.com/aruba-resort-and-casino-en.html.*

SPORTS AND
THE OUTDOORS

ON ARUBA YOU CAN HIKE a surreal arid outback and participate in every conceivable water sport, play tennis or golf, and horseback ride along the sea. But the big sport of note these days is beach tennis. Aruba has become the beach-tennis capital of the Caribbean, and Palm and Eagle Beaches host several tournaments, including one big annual international competition. As for water sports, the coolest new thing to do on Aruba is the thrilling jet-pack-over-water ride called Jetlev. They also offer hoverboard—an air-propelled skateboard over the waves—and jet blades, which are like ski boots on a board that jet-blast you into the air. Parasailing, banana boats, kayaking, paddleboarding, even yoga on paddleboard . . . you name it, Aruba has it. And this island has some of the world's best conditions for windsurfing and kiteboarding. In fact, it has produced world champions.

BICYCLING AND MOTORCYCLING

Biking is a great way to get around the island: the climate is perfect, and the trade winds help keep you cool. If you prefer to exert less energy while reaping the rewards of the outdoors, a scooter is a great way to whiz from place to place. Or let your hair down completely and cruise around on a Harley-Davidson.

ORGANIZED EXCURSIONS

Harley-Davidson Aruba Tours. Hog fans will adore this novel way to tour Aruba. On your own with a rental, or on one of their guided Harley-Davidson Madness group tours—a four-hour trip that takes only back roads to bring you the island's best sites—you will enjoy the open road like a rebel with this outfit. A motorcycle license and $1,000 deposit are required. ⊠ *L. G. Smith Blvd. 106, Oranjestad* ☎ *297/582–8660* ⊕ *www.harleydavidson-aruba.com.*

Rancho Notorious. One of Aruba's oldest tour operators, Rancho Notorious offers horseback riding for all levels and many different guided tours, including ATV outback adventures and mountain biking. Their adventures are a great way to experience the island's rugged, arid outback and scenic, rocky seasides where cars cannot venture. ⊠ *Boroncana, Noord* ☎ *297/586–0508* ⊕ *www.rancho notorious.com.*

RENTALS

There are plenty of dealers who will be happy to help you in your motoring pursuits.

Relatively flat, Aruba is the perfect biking destination.

BOWLING

★ **Fodor's Choice** **Dream Bowl Aruba.** Dream Bowl does it right with
FAMILY eight glow-in-the-dark bowling lanes, hip music, computerized scoring, and all kinds of special theme nights with
prizes. It's part of the larger entertainment emporium on
the top floors of the modern new Palm Beach Plaza that
includes a huge video arcade, a big modern sports bar,
billiard tables, a food court, and prize machines. ⊠ *Palm
Beach Plaza, Suite 310, L. G. Smith Blvd. 95, Palm Beach*
☎ *297/586–0809* ☺ *Daily 4–11 pm.*

Eagle Bowling Palace. Arubans love to bowl and often compete off-island. The newly modernized Eagle emporium is
close to the high-rise strip and has computerized lanes, a
snack bar, and a cocktail lounge. Equipment rentals and
group rates are available. ⊠ *Sasakiweg, Pos Abou, Oranjestad* ☎ *297/583–5038* ⊕ *www.facebook.com/pages/Eagle-
Bowling/188310420972* .

DAY SAILS

Aruba is not much of a "yachtie" destination; you won't
see a lot of sailboats, but you will see lots of luxury catamarans taking big groups of tourists out for a fun day of
party sailing, snorkeling tours, or sunset dinner cruises.
There are a few smaller private yacht charters available as
well. The weather is typically ideal, the waters are calm

8

Snorkeling from a replica pirate ship

and clear, and the trade winds are gentle, so there's never really a bad time to hit the waves.

Day sails usually take off from either De Palm Pier or Pelican Pier on Palm Beach. Many tour companies include pick-up and drop-off service at major resorts.

Mi Dushi. This romantic, two-masted ship ("My Sweetheart") offers daytime snorkeling trips that include breakfast, lunch, and drinks for $59 per person. It also offers popular sunset happy-hour cruises. ⊠ *Turibana Plaza, Noord 124, Noord* ☎ *297/586–2010* ⊕ *www.midushi.com.*

Octopus Sailing Charters. Captain Jethro Gesterkamp is at the helm for snorkel instruction and hosting aboard his small vessel, a 40-foot trimaran limited to 22 passengers—the experience is highly personal. Champagne brunch and sunset sails are also available. It's an economical alternative to some of the bigger snorkel tour operators. Private charters also available. ⊠ *Pelican Pier, Palm Beach* ☎ *297/593–3739* ⊕ *www.octopusaruba.com.*

Tranquilo Charters Aruba. Captain Mike Hagedoorn, a legendary Aruban sailor, has recently handed the helm over to his son Captain Anthony after 20 years of running the family business. Today, the *Tranquilo,* a 43-foot sailing yacht, still takes small groups of passengers to a secluded spot at Spanish Lagoon named "Mike's Reef" after his father, where no other snorkel trips venture. The lunch cruise to the south side always includes "Mom's famous Dutch pea soup," and they also do private charters for dinner sails and sailing trips around Aruba's less-explored coasts. Look for the red boat docked at the Renaissance Marina beside the Atlantis Submarine launch. ⊠ *Renaissance Marina, Oranjestad* ☎ *297/586–1418* ⊕ *www.tranquiloaruba.com.*

FISHING

Deep-sea catches here include anything from barracuda, tuna, and wahoo to kingfish, sailfish, and marlins, and a few skippered charter boats are available for half- or full-day excursions. Package prices vary, but typically include tackle, bait, and refreshments.

Teaser Charters. The expertise of the Teaser crew is matched by a commitment to sensible fishing practices, which include catch-and-release and avoiding ecologically sensitive areas. The company's two boats are fully equipped, and the crew seem to have an uncanny ability to locate the best fishing spots. Captain Kenny and Captain Milton run a thrilling expedition. ⊠ *Renaissance Marina, Oranjestad* ☎ *297/582– 5088* ⊕ *www.teasercharters.com.*

GOLF

Golf may seem incongruous on an arid island such as Aruba, yet there are several popular courses. Trade winds and the occasional stray goat add unexpected hazards.

8

The Links at Divi Aruba. This 9-hole course was designed by Karl Litten and Lorie Viola. The flat, par-36 layout stretches to 2,952 yards and features paspalum grass (best for seaside courses) and takes you past beautiful lagoons. It's a testy little course where water abounds, making accuracy more important than distance. Amenities include a golf school with professional instruction, a swing-analysis station, a driving range, and a two-story golf clubhouse with a pro shop. Two restaurants are available: Windows on Aruba for fine dining, and Mulligan's for a quick, casual lunch. ⊠ *Divi Village Golf & Beach Resort, J. E. Irausquin Blvd. 93, Oranjestad* ☎ *297/581–4653* ⊕ *www.divilinks.com* ⚑ *9 holes, 2952 yards, par 36.*

★ Fodor's Choice **Tierra del Sol.** Stretching out to 6,811 yards, this stunning course is situated on the northwest coast near the California Lighthouse and is Aruba's only 18-hole course. Designed by Robert Trent Jones Jr., Tierra del Sol combines

CLOSE UP

Sidney Ponson: Pitcher

When he was growing up in Aruba, Sidney Ponson loved sailing, scuba diving, and just about anything to do with the ocean. "My life was the beach," says Ponson, "before baseball." He started playing baseball when he was nine, even though the game was pretty difficult on an arid island where the fields are full of rocks. But employment on his uncle's boat taught him to work hard for what he wanted in life.

The pitcher signed with the minor leagues at 16, then was tapped by the Baltimore Orioles at 21. Hitting the big leagues involved lots of hard work—his grueling workouts lasted 7:30 am–1 pm and involved lifting weights, running, and throwing—but Ponson says it was worth it when he got the call to play. "It was 6:30 am, and I was on a road trip in a hotel in Scranton," he remembers. "They told me when to show up and said to be ready to play at 8:30."

Now Ponson is a free agent and spends much of his time in Aruba resting and visiting family and friends. Ponson used his status as a major leaguer to do some good for his island. He and fellow Aruban baseball player Calvin Maduro draft other professional baseball players, including Pedro Martinez and Manny Ramirez, to play in an annual celebrity softball game to raise funds for Aruba's Cas pa Hubentud, a home for underprivileged children.

He was awarded with the Order of Orange-Nassau by Queen Beatrix of the Netherlands in 2003.

Today Aruba has a new baseball star getting a lot of attention. Xander Jan Bogaerts plays as a shortstop/third baseman for the Boston Red Sox. He had the entire island on its feet when they won the World Series in 2013.

Aruba's native beauty—cacti and rock formations, stunning views, and good conditioning. Wind can also be a factor here on the rolling terrain as are the abundant bunkers and water hazards. Greens fees include a golf cart equipped with GPS and a communications system that allows you to order drinks for your return to the clubhouse. The fully stocked pro shop is one of the Caribbean's most elegant, with an extremely attentive staff. ⊠ *Caya di Solo 10, Malmokweg* ☎ *297/586–7800* ⊕ *www.tierradelsol.com* ⚑ *18 holes, 6811 yards, par 71.*

The California Lighthouse towers over Tierra del Sol golf course.

HIKING

Despite Aruba's arid landscape, hiking the rugged countryside will give you the best opportunities to see the island's wildlife and flora. Arikok National Wildlife Park is an excellent place to glimpse the real Aruba, free of the trappings of tourism. The heat can be oppressive, so be sure to take it easy, wear a hat, and have a bottle of water handy. Get maps and information at Arikok National Park Visitor Center.

Arikok National Park. There are more than 34 km (20 miles) of trails concentrated in the island's eastern interior and along its northeastern coast. Arikok Park is crowned by Aruba's second-highest mountain, the 577-foot Mt. Arikok, so you can also go climbing here.

Hiking in the park, whether alone or in a group led by guides, is generally not too strenuous. Look for different colors to determine the degree of difficulty of each trail. You'll need sturdy shoes to grip the granular surfaces and climb the occasionally steep terrain. You should also exercise caution with the strong sun—bring along plenty of water and wear sunscreen and a hat. On the rare occasion that it rains, the park should be avoided completely, as mud makes both driving and hiking treacherous. At the park's main entrance, the Arikok Park Visitor Center houses offices, restrooms, and food facilities. All visitors

Kayaking in a sheltered cove

must stop here upon entering, so that officials can manage traffic flow and distribute information on park rules and features. ☎ *297/582–8001* ⊕ *www.arubanationalpark.org.*

★ **Fodor's Choice** **Arikok Park Visitor Center.** Built in 2010, this massive, modern visitor center was constructed with the environment in mind by using sustainable materials and incorporating all kinds of eco-friendly practices to cool the interior. There are some live exhibits of Aruba's endemic creatures like the blue whiptail lizard, the endangered cascabel rattlesnake, and the Aruban cat-eye snake, and there's lots of information about other types of wildlife you might encounter on a hike or drive. There are also bathroom facilities, a souvenir shop, films about the flora and fauna, and a snack shop. Park rangers will take you on a guided tour of the wildlife and historical sites free of charge if you reserve a day in advance. Groups of up to 15 can be accommodated. The admission fee goes toward the conservation of the region. Note that you are not allowed to be in the park after sunset unless you have a camping permit. ✉ *San Fuego 71, Santa Cruz* ☎ *297/585–1234* ⊕ *www.aruba nationalpark.org/main* 💲 *$11* 🕒 *Daily 8–4.*

FAMILY **Donkey Sanctuary Aruba.** Aruba's donkeys were brought by the Spanish, but once they were no longer needed for transportation, they were basically left to fend for themselves in the wild. Unfortunately, many get sick while unattended, or injured from car traffic, and need human help; fortunately, there is a sanctuary for them run by Desiree Eldering and a team of dedicated volunteers. The nonprofit Donkey Sanctuary Aruba gives animals a safe place to heal or simply spend the rest of their years. The donkeys are friendly and love visitors—bring apples and carrots to really impress—and visitors can adopt a donkey at the sanctuary. Your donation goes to one specific donkey and pays for its care and feeding for a year. You can also adopt one from their website. ⌂ *Santa Lucia 41, Santa Cruz* ☎ *297/593–2933* ⊕ *main.arubandonkey.org/portal.*

FAMILY **Nature Sensitive Tours.** Eddy Croes, a former park ranger whose passion for nature is infectious, runs this outfitter with care. Groups are never larger than eight people, so you'll see as much detail as you can handle. The hikes are done at an easy pace and are suitable for just about any fitness level. Moonlight tours also available. If you'd rather not hike, Eddy also has a 4X4 monster-jeep guided tour of the arid outback for up to 20 people as well. ⌂ *Pos Chiquito 13E, Savaneta* ☎ *297/585–1594* ⊕ *www.nature sensitivetours.com.*

HORSEBACK RIDING

Ranches offer short jaunts along the beach or longer rides through the countryside and even to the ruins of an old gold mill. Riders of all experience levels will be thrilled that most of Aruba's horses are descendants of the Spanish Paso Fino (meaning "fine step"), which offer a super-smooth ride even at a trot!

8

FAMILY Fodor's Choice **Rancho Daimari.** This operation offers some of
★ the best horseback tours on Aruba. Choose from a trek to the incredible natural pool in the heart of Arikok National Park, or to a scenic and secret surfer beach. Tours are very family-friendly and accommodate all levels of riding skill. Complimentary return transportation is offered to hotels. Reservations are essential. ⌂ *Daimari Beach, Arikok Park* ☎ *297/586–6284* ⊕ *www.arubaranchodaimari.net.*

KAYAKING

Kayaking is a popular sport on Aruba, especially because the waters are so calm. It's a great way to explore the coast and the mangroves.

Aruba Kayak Adventure. Start with a quick lesson, and then get ready to paddle through caves and mangroves and

CLOSE UP

Wildlife Watching

Wildlife abounds on Aruba. Look for the cottontail rabbit: the black patch on its neck likens it to a species found in Venezuela, spawning a theory that it was brought to the island by pre-Columbian peoples. Wild donkeys, originally transported to the island by the Spanish, are found in more rugged terrain; sheep and goats roam freely throughout the island.

About 170 bird species make their home on Aruba year-round, and migratory birds temporarily raise the total to 300 species when they fly by in November and January. Among the highlights are the *trupiaal* (bright orange), the *prikichi* (a parakeet with a green body and yellow head), and the *barika geel* (a small, yellow-bellied bird with a sweet tooth—you may find one eating the sugar off your breakfast table). At Bubali Bird Sanctuary, on the island's western side, you can see various types of waterfowl, especially cormorants, herons, scarlet ibis, and fish eagles. Along the south shore brown pelicans are common. At Tierra del Sol golf course in the north you may glimpse the *shoco*, the endangered burrowing owl.

Lizard varieties include large iguanas, once hunted for use in local soups and stews (that practice is now illegal). Like chameleons, these iguanas change color to adapt to their surroundings—from bright green when foraging in the foliage (which they love to eat) to a brownish shade when sunning themselves in the dirt. The *pega pega*—a cousin of the gecko—is named for the suction pads on its feet that allow it to grip virtually any surface (*pega* means "to stick" in Papiamento). The *kododo blauw* (whiptail lizard) is one species that's unique to the island.

Until a few years ago, only two types of snakes were found on Aruba: the cat-eyed *santanero*, which isn't venomous, and the poisonous *cascabel*, a unique subspecies of rattlesnake that doesn't use its rattle. But because of human error, the boa has also ended up on Aruba and is actively hunted because it is an invasive species that has no natural predators on the island. Its growing numbers have been wreaking havoc on the island's native species like the shoco—recently named Aruba's national animal.

along the scenic coast for an exceptional half-day kayak trip. The tour makes a lunch stop at De Palm Island, where snorkeling is included as part of the $100 package. ✉ *J. W.*

Irausquin Blvd. 81B, Palm Beach ☎ *297/582–5520* ⊕ *www. arubakayak.com.*

Aruba Watersport Center. This family-run, full-service water-activity center is right on Palm Beach. They offer a comprehensive variety of adventures including diving, snorkeling, parasailing, Jet Ski and WaveRunner rentals, tubing, Hobie Cat sailing, stand-up paddleboarding, kayaking, wakeboard, and water skiing. Speedboat and bike rentals are available as well. ⊠ *L. G. Smith Blvd. 81B, Noord* ☎ *297/586–6613* ⊕ *www.arubawatersportscenter.com.*

KITEBOARDING

Thanks to constant trade winds, kiteboarding (also called kitesurfing) has become huge on this island. The sport involves gliding on and above the water on a small surf-board or wakeboard while hooked up to an inflatable kite. Windsurfing experience helps, and practice time on the beach is essential.

★ Fodor'sChoice **Aruba Active Vacations.** Located at the best spot on the island for optimum wind and wave conditions—this operation has been the go-to for many years as *the* place to learn windsurfing and kiteboarding. Their expert instructors ensure even first-timers are riding the waves in no time. Local alums of their school include world-class competitors like eight-time Women's World Champion windsurfer Sarah-Quita Offringa. They also offer mountain biking, stand-up paddleboarding, and the unique sport of "blokarting"—sail-powered land carting. ⊠ *North end, Fisherman's Huts Beach* ☎ *297/586–0989* ⊕ *www.aruba-active-vacations.com.*

MULTISPORT OUTFITTERS

There are a number of outfitters in Aruba that can handle nearly all your water- or land-based activities with guided excursions and rental equipment. Here is a list of a few of our favorites.

FAMILY Fodor'sChoice **De Palm Tours.** Aruba's premier tour company
★ covers every inch of the island on land and under sea, and they even have their own submarine (*Atlantis*) and semi-submarine (*Seaworld Explorer*) and their own all-inclusive private island destination (De Palm Island). Land exploration options include air-conditioned sightseeing bus tours, as well as rough and rugged outback jaunts by jeep safari to popular attractions like the natural pool. You can also do

off-road tours in an UTV (two-seater utility task vehicle) via their guided caravan trips. On the waves, their luxury catamaran *De Palm Pleasure* offers romantic sunset sails and snorkel trips that include an option to try SNUBA® (deeper snorkeling with an air-supplied raft) at Aruba's most famous shipwreck. De Palm also offers airport transfers. ⊠ *L. G. Smith Blvd. 142, Oranjestad* ☎ *297/582–4400* ⊕ *www.depalmtours.com.*

Pelican Adventures. In operation since 1984, this company arranges sailing and boating charters for fishing and exploring, as well as jeep adventures and guided excursions to Aruba's caves and historic sites. Scuba and snorkeling trips are available for divers of all levels. Novices start with mid-morning classes and then move to the pool to practice what they've learned; by afternoon they put their new skills to use at a shipwreck off the coast. Enjoy daytime snorkeling trips to two different reefs for about $47 per person. The company also offers sunset sails for $45 that can be combined with dinner at the Pelican Restaurant on Palm Beach. ⊠ *Pelican Pier, near Holiday Inn and Playa Linda hotels, Palm Beach* ☎ *297/586–3271* ⊕ *www.pelican-aruba.com.*

★ Fodor'sChoice **Red Sail Sports Aruba.** A dynamic company established almost 15 years ago and experts in the field of water-sports recreation, Red Sail offers excellent diving excursions, snorkel sails, sunset, sails, and full dinner sails. They even have their own sports equipment shop. They are also the original operator to introduce the cool new sport of Jetlev®—a personal jet pack over the water—and Jetblades—like roller blades on the waves. They also have the island's only certified instructors for these activities, and have recently opened their own beach-tennis club with expert instruction as well. There are locations in Palm Beach, Noord, and Oranjestad. ⊠ *Palm Beach* ☎ *297/586–1603* ⊕ *www.aruba-redsail.com.*

SCUBA DIVING AND SNORKELING

With visibility of up to 90 feet, the waters around Aruba are excellent for snorkeling and diving. Advanced and novice divers alike will find plenty to occupy their time, as many of the most popular sites—including some interesting shipwrecks—are found in shallow waters ranging 30–60 feet. Coral reefs covered with sensuously waving sea fans and eerie giant sponge tubes attract a colorful menagerie of sea life, including gliding manta rays, curious sea turtles, shy octopuses, and fish from grunts to groupers. Marine preservation is a priority on Aruba, and regulations by the Conference on International Trade in Endangered Species make it unlawful to remove coral, conch, and other marine life from the water.

In 2010, the Aruba Marine Park Foundation was established to protect the island's reefs and waters. It's a not-for-profit government organization, and they have been busy studying and defining the parameters that will best serve the island. One big issue they are tackling is the invasion of the non-native lionfish that threatens reefs throughout the Caribbean. If you spot a lionfish, report it to their organization, and do not touch it. The venom is poisonous and the sting very painful.

OPERATORS

Aruba Pro Dive. The fact that this is a small outfit that only caters to small groups (six max.) helps make each dive more personal, flexible, and unique. They also do night dives and all levels of PADI certification. ✉ *Ponton 90, Noord* ☎ *297/582–5520* ⊕ *www.arubaprodive.com.*

Dive Aruba. Resort courses, certification courses, and trips to interesting shipwrecks make Dive Aruba worth checking out. Small groups make it more personal. ✉ *Wilhelminastraat 8, Oranjestad* ☎ *297/582–7337* ⊕ *www.divearuba.com.*

★ Fodor'sChoice **JADS Dive Center.** J. P. Fang has moved his dive operation out to Baby Beach in San Nicolas where they have built an entire complex around the old Esso Social Club. There is a dive shop and snorkel equipment rental, and they have their own boats to charter for experienced divers. They also specialize in first-rate instruction for beginners. After the briefing, you head to Mangel Halto nearby for an easy shore dive that takes you to a little ship they scuttled to make an artificial reef. The complex also has washroom facilities, a playground, an outdoor shower, and a full beach bar/diner that has great local food, specialty cocktails, and sometimes live music. They are also planning a new dining spot next to an infinity pool there. ✉ *Seroe Colorado 245E, San Nicolas* ☎ *297/584–6070* ⊕ *www.jadsaruba.com.*

Native Divers Aruba. A small, personal operation, Native Divers Aruba specializes in PADI open-water courses. Ten different certification options include specialties like Multilevel Diver, Search & Recovery Diver, and Underwater Naturalist. Their boat schedule is also flexible and it's easy to tailor

DID YOU KNOW?

Whereas windsurfers stand on a large board connected to a sail, kiteboarders ride a much smaller board and are propelled by a kite that flies high in the air.

Diving one of Aruba's many wrecks

instruction to your specific needs. ⊠ *Marriott Surf Club, Palm Beach* ☎ *297/586–4763* ⊕ *www.nativedivers.com.*

S.E. Aruba Fly 'n Dive. One of the island's oldest diving operators, S.E. Aruba Fly 'n Dive offers a full range of PADI courses as well as many specialty courses like Nitrox Diver, Wreck Diver, and Deep Diver. They can also instruct you in rescue techniques and becoming an underwater naturalist. ⊠ *L. G. Smith Blvd. 1A, Oranjestad* ☎ *297/588-1150* ⊕ *www.se-aruba.com.*

Unique Sports of Aruba. Diving is the specialty here, with scads of one- and two-tank dives scheduled weekly, but they also offer a snorkel sail on a luxury catamaran and a SNUBA® (deep snorkeling with an oxygen raft), snorkel, and sail trip for those who are not yet certified. The staff teach beginner resort courses as well as a wide range of PADI courses, including Dive Master and Rescue. They depart from both the De Palm Pier and the Pelican Pier, depending on the trip. ⊠ *Radisson Aruba Resort & Casino, J. E. Irausquin Blvd. 81, Palm Beach* ☎ *297/586–0096, 297/586–3900* ⊕ *www.uniquesportsaruba.com.*

WEST-SIDE DIVE SITES

Antilla **Wreck.** This German freighter, which sank off the northwest coast near Malmok Beach, is popular with both divers and snorkelers. Scuttled during World War II not long after its maiden voyage, the 400-foot-long vessel—referred to by locals as "the ghost ship"—has large compartments. You can climb into the captain's bathtub, which sits beside the wreck, for a unique photo op. Lobster, angelfish, yellowtail, and other fish swim about the wreck, which is blanketed by giant tube sponges and coral. ⊠ *Malmok Beach.*

Black Beach. The clear waters just off this beach are dotted with sea fans. The area takes its name from the rounded black stones lining the shore. It's the only bay on the island's north coast sheltered from thunderous waves, making it a safe spot for diving.

Malmok Reef. Lobsters and stingrays are among the highlights at this bottom reef adorned by giant green, orange, and purple barrel sponges as well as leaf and brain coral. From here you can spot the *Debbie II,* a 120-foot barge that sank in 1992.

***Pedernales* Wreck.** During World War II this oil tanker was torpedoed by a German submarine. The U.S. military cut out the damaged centerpiece, towed the two remaining pieces to the States, and welded them together into a smaller vessel that eventually transported troops during the invasion of Normandy. The section that was left behind in shallow water is now surrounded by coral formations, making this a good site for novice divers. The ship's cabins, washbasins, and pipelines are exposed. The area teems with grouper and angelfish.

Skeleton Cave. Human bones found here (historians hypothesize that they're remains of ancient Arawak people) gave this dive spot its name. A large piece of broken rock forms the entrance where the cave meets the coast. ⊠ *Noord.*

EAST-SIDE DIVE SITES

***Captain Roger* Wreck.** A plethora of colorful fish swish about this old tugboat, which rests off the coast at Seroe Colorado. From shore you can swim to a steep coral reef.

FAMILY Fodor'sChoice **De Palm Island.** A must-do for a full or half-day
★ trip is a visit to this terrific little private island outpost full of incredible adventures for the entire family. Their all-inclusive offerings include snorkeling with giant neon blue parrotfish, a giant waterpark, banana-boat rides, salsa lessons, beach volleyball, zip-lining, and a massive all-you-can-eat buffet plus open bar and snack shack. For additional cost, you can also try SNUBA®—deep snorkeling with an oxygen raft—and children 4–7 can join their parents with their unique SNUBA Doo® set-up. Motor-

ized Power Snorkel is another fun undersea option. They also have Seatrek®—underwater walking tours with air-supplied helmets—and have added zip-lines over the water recently as well. There's also a small seaside spa on site. Complimentary bus transportation from all major hotels includes access to the island by water taxi. ⊠ *De Palm Island Way, Balashi* ☎ *297/522–4400* ⊕ *www.depalmtours.com.*

Jane Wreck. This 200-foot freighter, lodged in an almost vertical position at a depth of 90 feet, is near the coral reef west of De Palm Island. Night diving is exciting here, as the polyps emerge from the corals that grow profusely on the steel plates of the decks and cabins. Soft corals and sea fans are also abundant in the area. The current is strong, and this is for advanced divers only. ⊠ *De Palm Island.*

The Wall. From May to August, green sea turtles intent on laying their eggs abound at this steep-walled reef. You'll also spot groupers and burrfish swimming nearby. Close to shore, massive sheet corals are plentiful; in the upper part of the reef are colorful varieties such as black coral, star coral, and flower coral. Flitting about are brilliant damselfish, rock beauties, and porgies.

SKYDIVING

★ Fodor'sChoice **SkyDive Aruba.** There's nothing like the adrenaline rush when you are forced to jump out of a perfectly good airplane at 10,000 feet because you are attached to your instructor. You have no choice but to free-fall at 120 mph toward the island for 35 seconds until your chute opens, and then your downward journey has you floating to the sand in a little over five minutes. Tandem sky jumps over Aruba cost $250 per person. Afterward you can purchase a video of your courageous leap. Group discounts are available. ⊠ *Malmok Beach* ☎ *297/735–0654* ⊕ *www.skydivearuba.com.*

SUBMARINE EXCURSIONS

Atlantis Submarines. Enjoy the deep without getting wet in the *Atlantis*, a real U.S. Coast Guard–approved submarine run by De Palm Tours and operating on the island for over 25 years. The underwater reefs teem with marine life, and the 65-foot air-conditioned sub takes up to 48 passengers for a two-hour tour 95–150 feet below the surface along Barcadera. The company also owns the *Seaworld Explorer*, a semisubmersible that allows you to sit and view Aruba's marine habitat from five feet below the surface. (Children must be a minimum of

36 inches in height and at least four years old.) ✉ *Renaissance Marina, L. G. Smith Blvd. 82, Oranjestad* ☎ *297/583–6090* ⊕ *www.depalmtours.com/atlantis-submarines-expedition.*

TENNIS

Aruba Racquet Club. Aruba's winds make tennis a challenge even if you have the best of backhands. Although visitors can make arrangements to play at the resorts, priority goes to guests. Some private tennis clubs can also accommodate you, or you can try the facilities at the Aruba Racquet Club. Host to a variety of international tournaments, the club has eight courts (six lighted), as well as a swimming pool, an aerobics center, and a restaurant. ✉ *Rooisanto 21, Palm Beach* ☎ *297/586–0215* ⊕ *www.arc.aw.*

WINDSURFING

Aruba has all the right ingredients for windsurfing: trade winds that average 15 knots year-round (peaking May–July), a sunny climate, and perfect azure-blue waters. With a few lessons from a certified instructor, even novices will be jibing in no time. The southwestern coast's tranquil waters make it ideal for both beginners and intermediates, as the winds are steady but sudden gusts rare. Experts will find the waters of the Atlantic, especially around Grapefield and Boca Grandi beaches, more challenging; winds are fierce and often shift without warning. Some hotels include windsurfing in their water-sports packages, and most operators can help you arrange complete windsurfing vacations.

Every July sees the Hi-Winds Pro-Am Windsurfing Competition, attracting professionals and amateurs from around the world. There are divisions for women, men, juniors, masters, and grandmasters. Disciplines include slalom, course racing, long distance, and freestyle.

Sailboard Vacations. Complete windsurfing packages, including accommodations, can be arranged with Sailboard Vacations. Equipment rentals and week-long clinics also available. ✉ *L. G. Smith Blvd. 462, Malmok Beach* ☎ *800/252–1070* ⊕ *www.sailboardvacations.com.*

SHOPPING

SHOPPING CAN BE GOOD ON ARUBA. Although stores on the island often use the tagline "duty-free," the word "prices" is usually printed underneath in much smaller letters. The only real duty-free shopping is in the departure area of the airport. (Passengers bound for the United States should be sure to shop before proceeding through U.S. customs in Aruba.) Downtown stores do have very low sales tax, though, and some excellent bargains on high-end luxury items like gold, silver, gems, and high-end watches. Major credit cards are welcome everywhere, as are U.S. dollars. Aruba's souvenir and crafts stores are full of Dutch porcelains and figurines, as befits the island's heritage. Dutch cheese is a good buy, as are hand-embroidered linens and any products made from the native aloe vera plant—sunburn cream, face masks, or skin refreshers. Local arts and crafts run toward wood carvings and earthenware emblazoned with "Aruba: One Happy Island" and the like, but there are also many shops with unique Aruban items like designer apparel and fancy flip-flops and artwork if you know where to look. Don't try to bargain unless you are at a flea market or stall type of deal. Arubans consider it rude to haggle, despite what you may hear to the contrary.

HOW AND WHEN

A good way to survey the shops and malls in downtown Oranjestad is to hop aboard the free trolley that loops the downtown area. There are some interesting new offerings in the back streets now. Also the smaller malls along the strip, like the Village Square, have some unique artisan shops, as does Paseo Herencia, whose courtyard is the scene of nightly entertainment called "the Waltzing Waters."

There is late-night shopping in two locations. The first, in downtown Oranjestad at Renaissance Mall—a multilevel indoor/outdoor complex—stays open until 8 pm, and shops in the newer, modern, multilevel indoor shopping mall off the high-rise strip—Palm Beach Plaza—stay open until 10 pm. Many of the shops around Paseo Herencia also stay open late in high season. A few other shops that stay open late can be found in Alhambra's new mall as well.

ORANJESTAD AND ENVIRONS

MALLS AND MARKETPLACES

Caya G. F. Betico Croes. Oranjestad's original "Main Street" (behind the Renaissance Marina Resort) had been neglected, most cruise passengers preferring to stick to the front street near the marina where the high-end shops and open market souvenir stalls are. However, a recent massive renovation of the entire downtown area has breathed new life into the back streets, with pedestrian-only stretches, compact malls, and open resting areas. A free eco-trolley now loops all through downtown, allowing you to hop on and off to shop at all kinds of stores. Apparel, souvenirs, specialty items, sporting goods, cosmetics—you name it, you'll find it on this renewed street. ⊠ *Oranjestad.*

Renaissance Mall. Upscale name-brand fashion and luxury brands of perfume, cosmetics, leather goods is what you'll find in the array of 60 stores spanning two floors in this mall located within and underneath the Renaissance Marina Resort. You'll also find specialty items like cigars and designer shoes, plus high-end gold, silver, diamonds, and quality jewelry at low duty and no tax prices. Cafés and high-end dining, plus a casino and spa round out the offerings. Late-night shops stay open until 8 pm daily. ⊠ *Renaissance Marina Resort, L. G. Smith Blvd. 82, Oranjestad* ☎ *297/582–4622* ⊕ *www.shoprenaissancearuba.com.*

Renaissance Marketplace. Really more of a dining and gathering spot along the marina than a shopping complex, this is a lively spot with a few souvenir shops and specialty stores. There is also a modern cinema. But mostly it's full of eclectic dining emporiums and trendy cafés, and there's live music some weekends in their outdoor square. ⊠ *L. G. Smith Blvd. 9, Oranjestad* ⊕ *www.shoprenaissancearuba.com.*

Royal Plaza Mall. It's impossible to miss this gorgeous colonial-style, cotton-candy-color building with the big gold dome gracing the front street along the marina. It's one of the most photographed in Oranjestad. Three levels of shops—indoor and outdoor—make up this artsy arcade full of small boutiques, cigar shops, designer clothing outlets, gift and jewelry stores, and souvenir kiosks. Great dining and bars can be found here as well. ⊠ *L. G. Smith Blvd. 94, Oranjestad* ☎ *297/588–0351.*

9

CLOSE UP

Shopping That Gives Back

American ex-pat Jodi Tobman moved to Aruba some 20 years ago. Her chain of unique retail stores is well known among local and repeat visitors as having some of the most interesting finds on the island. But her stores are also different, because they are part of a community give-back program called Tikkun Olam, which loosely translates to "repair the world" in Hebrew.

The stores that participate in this program give back a percentage of their sales to community programs. At point of purchase, customers choose from a Community Menu, earmarking their choice for that store to donate to on their behalf. From Alzheimer's disease and cancer to autism, education for children, elderly support, abused women, and the arts—even youth sports— each store has its own menu of foundations to support.

Seeking out and patronizing these shops is worth it not only for the good feeling you get knowing you are giving back to your host island community

in some way, but also for the wares they sell. Tobman travels the globe seeking out unique products to stock the stores, always with an eye toward handcrafted or sustainable or arty concepts. Stores that participate in the program are the Caribbean Queen, the Lazy Lizard, the Coconut Trading Co., Caribbean Clothing Co., T.H. Palm & Company, and, recently, Juggling Fish. You will find them all over Aruba, and the items they stock run the gamut from avant-garde souvenirs and arty gifts to high-quality apparel and even housewares.

But one shop in particular also ensures that local female crafters and artisans get their due: the Caribbean Queen. Each month a different, locally based female artisan has her wares or products highlighted at the store as that month's chosen Caribbean Queen. On-site workshops with the artist in attendance also allow customers a peek behind the creative curtain. And the gorgeous items they create always make fabulous souvenirs for the folks back home.

SPECIALTY STORES

CIGARS

Cigar Emporium. The Cubans come straight from the climate-controlled humidor at Cigar Emporium. Choose from Cohiba, Montecristo, Romeo y Julieta, Partagas, and more. ✉ *Renaissance Mall, L. G. Smith Blvd. 82, Oranjestad* ☎ *297/582–5479.*

CLOTHING

Caribbean Clothing Co. This is the place to get stylishly outfitted for resort and vacation life right off the trolley stop in downtown Oranjestad. It has clothing for women and men, and all kinds of accessories as well, such as hats, shoes, and jewelry. A portion of the proceeds from all purchases goes back to community programs. ⊠ *Caya Betico Croes 32, Oranjestad* ☎ *297/592–7809* ⊕ *www.facebook.com/ CaribbeanClothingCo.*

Tommy Hilfiger. The activewear sold at Tommy Hilfiger makes this a great stop for a vacation wardrobe. A Tommy Jeans store is also here. They have also opened a new store in the Paseo Herencia Mall on the high-rise resort strip. ⊠ *Royal Plaza Mall, L. G. Smith Blvd. 94, Oranjestad* ☎ *297/583–8548.*

★ Fodor's Choice **Wulfsen & Wulfsen.** In business for over 50 years, this sophisticated shop offers elegant European fashions for both women and men, and footwear for men as well. Plus sizes are also available for the ladies, and their on-site tailor makes this a rare made-to-measure emporium on the island. ⊠ *Caya G. F. Betico Croes 52, Oranjestad* ☎ *297/582–3823.*

GIFTS AND SOUVENIRS

Artistic Boutique. The exclusive agents on the island for NAO by LLADRO collectible porcelain figurines and Aruba Lucky Stone, this little boutique also offers up a creative array of gold and silver jewelry, gems, pearls and fine watches, as well as unique giftware and decorative items like hand-crafted, local embroidery. ⊠ *Caya G. F. Betico Croes 23, Oranjestad* ☎ *297/581–3842.*

FOOD

Kong Hing Supercentre. This clean, orderly supermarket within walking distance of Druif Beach stocks all the typical grocery store staples, including fresh produce, meats, canned goods, baked goods, and a wide selection of beer, wine, and liquor. ⊠ *L. G. Smith Blvd. 152, Oranjestad* ☎ *297/582–5545* ⊙ *Mon.–Sat. 8–8, Sun. 9–1.*

★ Fodor's Choice **NUTS NUTS.** As you might have surmised by the name, they sell nuts! All kinds of nuts. But they also specialize in healthful foodstuffs such as grains, energy powders, dried fruits, condiments, and more. You can buy in bulk or in to-go packs. They also have lots of organic, gluten-free, vegan, and high-protein choices and healthful versions of snacks, shakes, teas, smoothies, and even parfaits, plus seriously decadent-tasting sugar-free desserts and baked goods. Gluten-free baking and pancake mixes are also available. ✉ *Engelandstraat 2, #2, Oranjestad* ☎ *297/587–6887* ⊕ *www.nuts-nuts.com* ✆ *Closed Sun.*

JEWELRY

Colombian Emeralds. A trusted international jewelry dealer specializing in emeralds, this outlet also has a top-notch selection of diamonds, sapphires, tanzanite, rubies, ammolite, pearls, gold, semiprecious gems, luxury watches, and more at very competitive prices. A highly professional and knowledgeable staff adds to their credibility. ✉ *Renaissance Mall, L. G. Smith Blvd. 82, Oranjestad* ☎ *297/583–6238* ⊕ *www.colombianemeralds.com.*

★ **Fodor's**Choice **Diamonds International.** One of the pioneer diamond retailers in the Caribbean with over 130 stores throughout the chain, the Aruba outlet has been operating in the same spot since 1997. They are well known for their expertise, selection, quality, and competitive prices on diamonds, and they also sell high-end timepieces. The founders of Diamonds International are both graduates of the Gemological Institute of America. ✉ *Port of Call Marketplace, L. G. Smith Blvd. 17, Oranjestad* ☎ *800/515–3935* ⊕ *www.diamondsinternational.com.*

Gandelman Jewelers. One of the island's premier jewelers, family-run Gandelman's is Aruba's official Rolex retailer and the exclusive agent for names like Cartier, Patek Philippe, David Yurman, and Bulgar. They have three stores on Aruba: one in the Aruba Marriott and one in the Aruba Hyatt, plus their flagship store, which has a Cartier Boutique, in the upscale Renaissance Mall in Oranjestad. They also have watches by TechnoMarine, Victorinox Swiss Army, and Brera, and jewelry by Pomellato, Mimi, Lisa Nik, and Jemma Wynn. ✉ *Renaissance Mall, L. G. Smith Blvd. 82, Oranjestad* ☎ *297/529–9920* ✆ *Mon.–Sat. 10–8.*

LEATHER GOODS

Gucci. If you get lucky, you can catch one of the year's big sales (one is held the first week in December, the other the first week in February) at Gucci, when prices are slashed on handbags, luggage, wallets, shoes, watches, belts, and ties. ✉ *Renaissance Mall, L. G. Smith Blvd. 82, Oranjestad* ☎ *297/583–3952.*

Beyond T-Shirts and Key Chains

You can't go wrong with baseball caps, refrigerator magnets, beer mugs, sweatshirts, T-shirts, key chains, and other local logo merchandise. You won't go broke buying these items, either. But do try to look for items actually made on Aruba rather than imported from China.

Budget for a major purchase. If souvenirs are all about keeping the memories alive in the long haul, plan ahead to shop for something really special—a work of art, a rug or something else handcrafted, or a major accessory for your home. One major purchase will stay with you far longer than a dozen tourist trinkets.

Add to your collection. Whether antiques, used books, salt-and-pepper shakers, or ceramic frogs are your thing, start looking in the first day or two. Chances are you'll want to scout around and then go back to some of the first shops you visited before you hand over your credit card.

Get guarantees in writing. Is the vendor making promises? Ask him or her to put them in writing.

Anticipate a shopping spree. Pack a large tote bag in your suitcase in case you need extra space. If you think you might buy breakables, include a length of bubble wrap. Don't fill your suitcase to bursting before you leave home. Or include some old clothing that you can leave behind to make room for new acquisitions.

Know before you go. Study prices at home on items you might consider buying while you're away. Otherwise you won't recognize a bargain when you see one.

Plastic, please. Especially if your purchase is pricey and you're looking for authenticity, it's always smart to pay with a credit card. If a problem arises later and the merchant can't or won't resolve it, the credit-card company may help you out.

LUXURY GOODS

Aruba Trading Company. Established in 1933, and located in the gorgeous Dutch colonial structure known as "La Casa Amarilla" (the Yellow House) in downtown Oranjestad, this shop specializes in fine perfumes, high-end cosmetics, and personal-care products. They also have beauty specialists and makeup artists on site. ⊠ *Caya G. F. Betico Croes 12, Oranjestad* ☎ *297/582–2602* ⊕ *www.arubatrading.com.*

★ **Fodor's Choice** **Little Switzerland.** With five stores on the island—most in high-rise resorts and the original location in downtown Royal Plaza Mall—these outlets specialize in designer jewelry and upscale timepieces by big-name designers like TAGHeuer, David Yurman, Breitling, Roberto Coin, Chopard, Pandora, Tiffany & Co., and Cartier Movado, Omega, and John Hardy. ⊠ *Royal Plaza Mall, L. G. Smith Blvd. 94, Oranjestad* ☎ *284/809–5560* ⊕ *www.little switzerland.com.*

PERFUMES

Aruba Trading Company, Little Switzerland, and Maggy's are also known for their extensive fragrance offerings (⇨ *see Luxury Goods, above*).

J.L. Penha & Sons. Originating in Curacao in 1865, Penha has branched out throughout the Caribbean and has seven stores on Aruba. The largest is right next to the Renaissance Hotel. Known for good prices on high-end perfumes, cosmetics, skincare products, and, more recently, eyewear and fashion. Brand and designer names include MAC, Lancôme, Estée Lauder, Clinique, Chanel, Dior, Montblanc, and Victoria's Secret to name just a few. Their newest store is in Plaza Daniel Leo downtown. ⊠ *Caya G. F. Betico Croes 11/13, Oranjestad* ☎ *297/582–4160, 297/582–4161* ⊕ *www.jlpenha.com.*

Maggy's. The flagship Maggy's is in downtown Oranjestad, but there are four more stores and two salons on the island. They are Aruba's premier emporium for duty-free perfumes, cosmetics, and name-brand skin-care items. ⊠ *Renaissance Mall, L. G. Smith Blvd. 9, Lot 3-B, Oranjestad* ☎ *297/583–6108* ⊕ *www.maggysaruba.com* ⊙ *Mon.–Sat. 10–7, Sun. 10–2.*

9

SPAS

★ Fodor's Choice **New Image Beauty-Spa & Health Center Aruba.** Boasting the only hammam on Aruba, this new full-service spa and health and beauty center in the Divi Aruba Golf Resort offers the most comprehensive range of services on the island. Beyond the typical spa menu of massages, facials, wraps, and mani-pedis, they also offer foot reflexology, detoxification, permanent makeup, cosmetology, hair removal, injectables, and hairdressing. The concept is built around organic and natural products whenever possible, and the ambience is warm and inviting, with a champagne welcome and a highly personable and competent staff. ⊠ *Divi Village Golf Resort, J. E. Irausquin Blvd., Oranjestad* ☎ *297/582–2288* ⊕ *www.newimagearuba.com.*

MANCHEBO AND DRUIF BEACHES

SPECIALTY STORES

GIFTS AND SOUVENIRS

Alhambra Mall. There's an eclectic array of shops and dining in the Alhambra Mall with the casino as its focal point. Dotted with designer retail stores like The Lazy Lizard and the Aruba Aloe outlet, and a full-service market and deli, the alfresco mall also has fast-food outlets like Juan Valdez Coffee Shop, Baskin Robbins, and Subway. Fusions Wine & Tapas Bar and popular new eateries Hollywood Smokehouse and Twist of Flavors round out the dining options. There's also a small full-service spa. ⊠ *L. G. Smith Blvd. 47, Manchebo Beach* ☎ *297/583–5000.*

EAGLE BEACH

SPECIALTY STORES

FOOD

Ling & Sons IGA Super Center. Always a family-owned and -operated grocery company, Ling & Sons adopted the IGA-brand supermarket style and moved to a bigger, better location close to downtown Oranjestad with all the goods you would expect in an IGA back home. In addition to a wide variety of foods, there's a bakery, a deli, a butcher, and a well-stocked "liquortique." You can also order your groceries online to be delivered to your hotel room. Ask about their VIP card for discounts. ⊠ *Schotlandstraat 41, Eagle Beach* ☎ *297/583–2370* ⊕ *www.lingandsons.com/home.do* ⊗ *Mon.–Sat. 8 am–9 pm, Sun. 9–6.*

PALM BEACH AND NOORD

MALLS

★ Fodor'sChoice **Palm Beach Plaza.** Aruba's most modern multi-story mall has three floors of shops offering fashion, tech, electronics, jewelry, souvenirs, and more. Entertainment includes, glow-in-the-dark bowling, a modern video arcade, a sports bar, and the main-floor indoor courtyard is often used for local festivals and events like fashion shows. Dining includes a food court and stand-alone restaurants and bars, and there are also modern air-conditioned cinemas and a spa within. ⊠ *L. G. Smith Blvd. 95, Palm Beach Plaza Mall, Noord* ☎ *297/586–0045* ⊕ *www.palmbeachplaza.com.*

FAMILY Fodor'sChoice **Paseo Herencia.** A gorgeous old-fashioned colo-
★ nial style courtyard and clock tower encases souvenir and specialty shops, cinemas, dining spots, cafés, and bars in this low-rise alfresco mall just off Palm Beach. Famous for its "liquid fireworks" shows when three times a night neon-lit water fountains "waltz" to music in a choreographed dance. Visitors can enjoy it for free from an outdoor amphi-theater where many cultural events also take place. There's also a fancy carousel for children and a trendy bar with an outside dipping pool with neon-lit chairs that constantly change colors. A must-visit—if not for the shopping—then for the water show alone. ⊠ *J. E. Irausquin Blvd. 382, Palm Beach* ☎ *297/586–6533* ⊕ *www.paseoherencia.com.*

★ Fodor'sChoice **Super Food Plaza.** So much more than simply a grocery store, this massive emporium of food and services rivals many big-city super-centers. Everything from fresh produce, a butcher and deli, fresh fish and seafood, an on-site bakery, a pharmacy, beauty and health products, sit-down snack shops, and even a toy shop are a few of the surprises you will find here. Prices are just a tad higher than in North America, but quality is good. ⊠ *Bubali 141-A, Noord* ☎ *297/522–2000* ⊕ *www.superfoodaruba.com* ⊘ *Mon.–Sat. 8–8, Sun. 9–6.*

SPECIALTY STORES

GIFTS AND SOUVENIRS

The Coconut Trading Co. The ultimate gift shop features hand-crafted treasures by local artisans, including sterling jewelry, precious gems, sea glass, turquoise, and freshwater pearls. Home-décor gifts include photo frames, candleholders, dishware and glassware, curios, and all kinds of avant-garde items. A portion of the proceeds from all purchases goes back to community programs. ⊠ *L. G. Smith Blvd. 99, Palm Beach* ☎ *297/586–2930* ⊕ *www.facebook.com/ TheCoconutTradingCo.*

★ Fodor'sChoice **The Juggling Fish.** The sign outside says "Distinc-tive Swimwear and Unique Souvenirs," and this whimsical shop just off the sand on Palm Beach at Playa Linda Resort certainly has that. There's a very special selection of swim-wear for the entire family, and some of the most creative and unique souvenirs on the island, including avant-garde

Many Aruba resorts have their own spas providing body treatments and massages.

jewelry and handcrafted items and accessories. The staff are warm and welcoming, and a portion of all purchases goes to community programs through a special give-back program. ✉ *Playa Linda Beach Resort, Palm Beach* 📞 *297/586–4999* 🌐 *www.facebook.com/TheJugglingFishAruba.*

★ Fodor's Choice **The Mask.** This shop specializes in original masks and crafty items called Mopa-Mopa Art. Originating with the Quillacingas Indians of Ecuador and Colombia, the art is made from the bud of the mopa-mopa tree, boiled down into a resin, colored with dyes, and applied to carved mahogany and other woods like cedar. Masks, jewelry boxes, coasters, whimsical animal figurines, and more make wonderfully unique gifts and souvenirs. The masks are also believed to ward off evil spirits. ✉ *Paseo Herencia, J. E. Irausquin Blvd. 382-A, Local C017, Palm Beach* 📞 *297/586–2900* 🌐 *www.mopamopa.com.*

★ Fodor's Choice **T.H. Palm & Company.** With an eclectic collection of upscale and exclusive items curated from all over the world by the owner, this unique boutique offers everything from top-line fashions for men and women, including footwear, handcrafted jewelry, and accessories, to art deco items for the home and novelty gifts for pets. It's a very popular spot for locals to buy gifts as well as for visitors to buy one-of-a-kind souvenirs. A portion of all purchases goes to the community through a special give-back program.

✉ *J. E. Irausquin Blvd. 87, Palm Beach* ☎ *297/586–6898* ⊕ *www.facebook.com/T.H.PalmAndCompany.*

JEWELRY

★ **Fodor's** Choice **Caribbean Queen.** At this unique boutique dedicated to the spirit of West Indian women, the jewelry, adornments, and fashionable accessories are mostly handcrafted and often beautiful works of art in their own right. As a way to promote locally made products, a creator/crafter in the store demonstrates how the items are made with special workshops as the "Caribbean Queen" of the month, and a portion of all purchases goes to local charities and nonprofit foundations. They also sell handbags, belts, hats, and shoes. ✉ *Palm Beach Plaza, L. G. Smith Blvd. 95, #123, Palm Beach* ☎ *297/586-8737* ⊕ *www. caribbean-queen.com.*

SPAS

★ **Fodor's** Choice **Body & Soul Spa.** Tierra del Sol's luxury villa and home rentals are typically the visiting-celebrity choice, and their Robert Trent Jones II–designed golf course is where serious golfers play. So it's no surprise that this spa blends into the entire upscale-luxury scene here perfectly. One highlight is the private couples whirlpool where romantics can canoodle with champagne in peace. They also have an interesting new sea-sand detox skin treatment. But most come here for the high-end massages, wraps, scrubs, and skin treatments, and there is also a full hair and nail-care salon. Spa guests are welcome to use the fitness center and lounge by the cliffside pool looking out at the California Lighthouse. ✉ *Caya di Solo 10, Noord* ☎ *297/586–7800* ⊕ *www.tierradelsol.com/en/body-soul-spa-fitness.*

★ **Fodor's** Choice **Larimar Spa and Salon.** Larimar is a large and soul-soothing full-service spa with Caribbean-inspired accents. Specializing in the use ESPA's natural products, they offer a comprehensive range of treatments from scrubs and wraps to facials for both women and men. All massages can be enjoyed in lovely seaside cabanas as well. Nail and hair salons are also on site. ✉ *Radisson Aruba Resort & Casino, J. E. Irausquin Blvd. 81, Palm Beach* ☎ *297/586–6555* ⊕ *www.radisson.com.*

Mandara Spa. The Aruba Marriott's Mandara Spa was created along a Balinese theme and offers some signature Balinese specialties like the *boreh* (a traditional warm healing pack of special spices), followed by a wrap using local

9

Aruban aloe and cucumber. They have a wide range of treatments and a full-service salon that can accommodate wedding parties. They also cater well to honeymooners, with some very special packages and private couples rooms with extra-large whirlpool baths or Vichy showers. ⊠ *L. G. Smith Blvd. 101, Palm Beach* ☎ *297/520–6750* ⊕ *www. marriott.com/hotels/hotel-information/fitness-spa-services/ auaar-aruba-marriott-resort-and-stellaris-casino.*

Nafanny Spa. Massage therapist Fanny Lampe's home and yard in Alto Vista provide a peaceful and picturesque backdrop for the pure relaxation to come. Thai, Swedish, bamboo, and hot-stone massages are all on offer as are various treatments, including a 90-minute wine-therapy session and numerous facial treatments using soothing botanicals designed to ease away impurities and stress lines. The location is a bit remote, but the tranquil setting makes that something of an advantage—Fanny will often pick up clients at their resort. Daily yoga classes are also offered. Though not offered as a package, customized half- and full-day spa bundles can be created. Nafanny Spa isn't the fanciest on the island, but the individual attention is unbeatable and so are the prices. ⊠ *Alto Vista 39F, Noord* ☎ *297/586–3007* ⊕ *www.nafanny.com.*

Okeanos. The ocean provides the backdrop for this spa in the Renaissance, which has its own massage cove that seems a world apart from the rest of the resort. Outdoor massages and showers help to bring the calming effects of nature into the treatments. In addition to the usual assortment of massages and wraps, the spa also offers both anti-cellulite and anti-aging treatments. There are a huge number of packages available, including one that combines Swedish massage with a meal served by your own butler. Pampering doesn't get much better than this. There are also optional packages to use the spa services at the Cove Spa located on the resort's private island. ⊠ *Renaissance Aruba Resort & Casino, L. G. Smith Blvd. 82, Palm Beach* ☎ *297/583–6000* ⊕ *www.renaissancearubaspa.com.*

★ Fodor's Choice **Pure Indulgence Spa.** The same people who own the well-established Indulgence by the Sea Spa have created a new "Pure" spa at Divi Aruba Phoenix Resort in keeping with the Pure Beach and Pure Ocean Divi branding. With gorgeous new rooms and couples suites, they offer Mircosilk Hydrotherapy baths and premium Hansgrohe

Raindance rain showers, and the facility features top-of-the-line treatments and many extras, including beach massages. A new mani-pedi loft boasts spectacular sea views as well, and they are well equipped to accommodate bridal parties. ⊠ *Palm Beach* ☎ *297/583–0083* ⊕ *www.facebook.com/pureindulgencespa.*

The Ritz-Carlton Spa. Natural elements are the main theme at this upscale new spa with signature treatments revolving around earth, sky, fire, and water. Local and natural ingredients have been incorporated wherever possible, such as Aruban honey in the Candela Deseo scrub, the Dushi Terra treatment that uses local black stones for massage, and the Awa awakening water treatment that infuses oils from local flowers for massage. They also offer a unique massage in a hammock, and they have soothing hydrotherapy options on site. The spa has 13 treatment rooms and an adjoining fitness center with daily classes, including yoga. ⊠ *The Ritz-Carlton, L. G. Smith Blvd. 107, Noord* ☎ *297/527–2222* ⊕ *www.ritzcarlton.com/en/Properties/Aruba/Spa/Default.htm.*

ZoiA Spa. It's all about indulgence at the Hyatt's upscale spa named after the Papiamento word for balance. Gentle music and the scent of botanicals make the world back home fade into the background. Newly arrived visitors to the island can opt for the jet-lag massage that combines reflexology and aromatherapy and those with the budget and the time for a full day of relaxation can opt for the Serene package. There's even a mother-to-be package available. Island brides can avail themselves of a full menu of beauty services ranging from botanical facials (using local ingredients) to a full makeup job for the big day. The Pure High Tea package offers a delicious assortment of snacks and teas along with an hour of treatments. ⊠ *Hyatt Regency Aruba Beach Resort & Casino, J. E. Irausquin Blvd. 85, Palm Beach* ☎ *297/586–1234* ⊕ *www.aruba.hyatt.com.*

DIVI BEACH

SPAS

Indulgence by the Sea Spa. The spa/salon serving the Divi Aruba and Tamarijn all-inclusives offers a wide range of premium services. Begin your journey to relaxation with a rose-filled, pure essential-oil footbath, cold cucumbers for the eyes, and a lavender heat wrap. Products are organic and natural—all handpicked and tested by the owner. A full range of massages includes a couples sea escape in a private cabana. The spa portion is at Divi Aruba, and the salon that specializes in bridal paxrties for special-occasion hair and makeup is at Tamarijn. ✉ *J. E. Irausquin Blvd. 45, Divi beach* ☎ *297/583–0083* ⊕ *www.spaaruba.com.*

TRAVEL SMART
ARUBA

GETTING HERE AND AROUND

Aruba is a small island, so it's virtually impossible to get lost when exploring. Most activity takes place in and around Oranjestad or in the two main hotel areas, which are designated as the "low-rise" and "high-rise" areas. Main roads on the island are generally excellent, but getting to some of the more secluded beaches or historic sites will involve driving on unpaved tracks. Though Aruba is an arid island, there are occasional periods of heavy rain, and it's best to avoid exploring the national park or other wilderness areas during these times, since roads can become flooded, and muddy conditions can make driving treacherous.

▮ AIR TRAVEL

Aruba is 2½ hours from Miami, 4½ hours from New York, and 9½ hours from Amsterdam. The flight from New York to San Juan, Puerto Rico, takes 3½ hours; from Miami to San Juan it's 1½ hours; and from San Juan to Aruba it's just over an hour. Shorter still is the ¼- to ½-hour hop (depending on whether you take a prop or a jet plane) from Curaçao to Aruba.

Airline-Security Issues Transportation Security Administration. The TSA has answers for almost every question that might come up. ⊕ *www.tsa.gov.*

AIRPORTS

The island's Reina Beatrix International Airport (AUA) has been recently revamped and is equipped with thorough security, lots of flight displays, and state-of-the-art baggage-handling systems, shopping, and food-and-drink emporiums.

Airport Information Aeropuerto Internacional Reina Beatrix. This refreshed, clean, and modern airport has lots of food and drink, banks/ATMs, duty-free shopping, and lounging areas, including a VIP lounge. Check their website for updated flight information, transportation options, and alerts. ✉ *Wayaca z/n* ☎ *297/524–2424* ⊕ *www.airportaruba.com.*

GROUND TRANSPORTATION

A taxi from the airport to most hotels takes about 20 minutes. It'll cost $22 to get to the hotels along Eagle Beach, $25 to the high-rise hotels on Palm Beach, and $18 to the hotels downtown (rates are a few dollars higher at night). You'll find a taxi stand right outside the baggage-claim area. Aruba taxis are not metered; they operate on a flat rate by destination. See ⊕ *www.aruba.com/things-to-do/taxis-and-limousine-services* for more information on rates.

For a pdf of rates see ⊕ *www.aruba.com/sigma/Aruba_Taxi_Fares.pdf.*

FLIGHTS

Many airlines fly nonstop to Aruba from several cities in North America; connections will usually be at a U.S. airport.

NONSTOP FLIGHTS

There are nonstop flights from Atlanta (Delta), Boston (American, JetBlue, US Airways), Charlotte (US Airways), Chicago (United), Fort Lauderdale (Spirit), Houston (United), Miami (American), Newark (United), New York–JFK (American, Delta, JetBlue), Philadelphia (US Airways), and Washington, D.C.–Dulles (United). Southwest Airlines has begun flights to Aruba from Baltimore and Houston as well. Seasonal nonstops from major Canadian cities are available from WestJet and Air Canada and charter airlines like Sunwing and Air Transat.

Because of pre-U.S. customs clearance, you really need three hours before departure from Aruba's airport. Beyond typical check-in lines—unless you check in online and do not have baggage—you must go through two separate security checks and customs as well, and sometimes even random baggage checks. The entire procedure takes a lot of time, and there are not often enough customs agents on duty to handle all the traffic, especially on weekends. So be there early. The good news is that you do not have to deal with customs in the United States on the other end. The airport departure tax is typically included in the price of your ticket.

Airline Contacts Air Canada. Direct flights are available from

Toronto only. ☎ 888/247–2262 in North America ⊕ www.air-canada.com. **American Airlines** ☎ 297/582–2700 on Aruba, 800/433–7300 ⊕ www.aa.com. **Delta Airlines** ☎ 297/800–1555 on Aruba, 800/221–1212 for U.S. reservations, 800/241–4141 for international reservations ⊕ www.delta.com. **JetBlue** ☎ 800/538–2583 ⊕ www.jetblue.com. **KLM** ☎ 5999/868–0195 on Aruba, 31/20–4–747–747 in Amsterdam ⊕ www.klm.com. **Spirit Airlines** ☎ 800/772–7117 ⊕ www.spiritair.com. **United Airlines** ☎ 297/562–9592 on Aruba, 800/538–2929 in North America ⊕ www.united.com. **US Airways** ☎ 800/455–0123 for U.S. and Canada reservations, 800/622–1015 for international reservations ⊕ www.usairways.com.

▎ BUS TRAVEL

Arubus N.V. is Aruba's public bus fleet. They are clean, well maintained, air-conditioned, and regularly scheduled, and provide a safe, economical way to travel along the resort beaches all the way to the downtown Oranjestad main terminal. They stop at almost all major resorts and offer a great way to hop into town for groceries to bring back to your hotel without taking expensive taxis. They run until fairly late at night and later on weekends, and if you are going to take them a lot, you are best off purchasing a pass called a Smart Card. They also give change if you do not have the exact fare, but not on big bills, though they do accept U.S. funds. Return fare is $4, but check for updated information on rates, schedules, and routes on their website, because they do change.

Contacts **Arubus** ⊕ *www.arubus. com.*

▌ CAR TRAVEL

Most of Aruba's major attractions are fairly easy to find, and there are great maps and apps all over the island to find out-of-the-way spots. International traffic signs and Dutch-style traffic signals (with an extra light for a turning lane) can be confusing, though, if you're not used to them; use extreme caution, especially at intersections, until you grasp the rules of the road.

GASOLINE

Gas prices average a little more than $1.25 per liter (roughly a quarter of a gallon), which is reasonable by Caribbean standards. Stations are plentiful in and near Oranjestad, San Nicolas, and Santa Cruz, and near the major highrise hotels on the western coast. All take cash, and most take major credit cards. Unlike in the United States, gas prices aren't posted prominently, since they're fixed and the same at all stations.

PARKING

There aren't any parking meters in downtown Oranjestad, and finding an open spot is very difficult, especially now that a lot of the downtown area is closed to vehicular traffic because of the eco-trolley and new pedestrian malls, but if you are lucky, there is free parking in the Renaissance Marketplace.

RENTAL CARS

In Aruba you must meet the minimum age requirements of each rental service. (Budget, for example, requires drivers to be over 25; Avis, over 23; and Hertz, over 21) A signed credit-card slip or a cash deposit of $500 is required. Rates for unlimited mileage run $35–$65 per day, with local agencies generally offering lower rates. Insurance is available starting at about $10 per day. Try to make reservations before arriving, and opt for a four-wheel-drive vehicle if you plan to explore the island.

Contacts **Avis** ⊠ *330 J. E. Irausquin Blvd., Oranjestad* ☎ *297/586–2181, 800/522–9696* ⊕ *www.avis.com* ⊠ *Airport* ☎ *297/582–5496.* **Budget** ⊠ *Camacuri 10, Oranjestad* ☎ *297/582–8600, 800/472–3325* ⊕ *www.budget.com.* **Economy** ⊠ *Bushiri 27, Oranjestad* ☎ *297/582–0009* ⊕ *www.economy aruba.com.* **Hertz** ⊠ *Sabana Blanco 35, near airport* ☎ *297/582–1845, 800/654–3001* ⊕ *www.arubarentcar. com/component/option,com_front page/Itemid,1.* **Thrifty** ⊠ *Wayaca 33-F, Oranjestad* ☎ *297/583–4042* ⊕ *www.thriftycarrentalaruba.com* ⊠ *Airport* ☎ *297/583–4902.*

RENTAL-CAR INSURANCE

Everyone who rents a car wonders whether the insurance that the rental companies offer is worth the expense. No one—including us—has a simple answer. If you own a car, your personal auto insurance may cover a rental to some degree, though not all policies protect you abroad; always read your policy's fine print. If you don't have auto insurance, then seriously consider buying the collision- or loss-damage waiver (CDW or LDW) from the car-rental company, which eliminates your liability for damage to the car. Some credit cards offer CDW coverage, but it's usually supplemental to your own insurance and rarely covers SUVs, minivans, or luxury models. If your coverage is secondary, you may still be liable for loss-of-use costs from the car-rental company. But no credit-card insurance is valid unless you use that card for *all* transactions, from reserving to paying the final bill. It's sometimes cheaper to buy insurance as part of your general travel-insurance policy.

ROADSIDE EMERGENCIES

Discuss with the rental-car agency what to do in the case of an emergency. Make sure you understand what your insurance covers and what it doesn't; let someone at your accommodation know where you're heading and when you plan to return. If you find yourself stranded, hail a taxi or speak to the locals, who may have some helpful advice about finding your way to a phone or a bus stop. Keep emergency numbers with you, just in case. Because Aruba is such a small island, you should never panic if you have car trouble; it's likely you'll be within relatively easy walking distance of a populated area.

ROAD CONDITIONS

Aside from the major highways, the island's winding roads are poorly marked (although the situation is slowly improving). Keep an eye out for rocks and other debris when driving on remote roads. When in the countryside, also keep your eyes open for wild goats and donkeys that might wander onto the road.

RULES OF THE ROAD

Driving here is on the right side of the road, American-style. Despite the laid-back ways of locals, when they get behind the steering wheel they often speed and take liberties with road rules, especially outside the more heavily traveled Oranjestad and hotel areas. Keep a watchful eye for passing cars and for vehicles coming out of side roads. Speed limits are rarely posted, but the maximum speed is 60 kph (40 mph) and 40 kph (25 mph) through settlements. Speed limits and the use of seat belts are enforced.

▮ TAXI TRAVEL

There's a dispatch office at the airport, and you can get taxis at all major resorts. Just ask someone at the front desk or the bellman. Rates are fixed (i.e., there are no meters; the rates are set by the government and displayed on a chart) and are posted on the Aruba Tourism Authority website, though you and the driver should agree on the fare before your ride begins. Add $2 to the fare after midnight and $2–$4 on Sunday and holidays. An hour-long island tour costs about $40 for up to four people. Rides into town from Eagle Beach run about $10; from Palm Beach, about $11.

Contact Airport Taxi Dispatch
☎ *297/582–2116.*

ESSENTIALS

▍ ACCOMMODATIONS

Hotels collect 9.5% in taxes (2% of which goes to marketing to tourists) on top of a typical 11% service charge, for a total of 20.5%. An additional $3-per-day Environmental Levy was added in 2013. Most hotels and other lodgings require you to give your credit-card details before they'll confirm your reservation. If you don't feel comfortable emailing this information, ask if you can fax it (some places even prefer faxes). However you book, get confirmation in writing and have a copy of it handy when you check in.

Be sure you understand the hotel's cancellation policy. Some places allow you to cancel without any kind of penalty—even if you prepaid to secure a discounted rate—if you cancel at least 24 hours in advance. Others require you to cancel a week in advance or penalize you the cost of one night. Small inns and bed-and-breakfasts are most likely to require you to cancel far in advance. Most hotels allow children under a certain age to stay in their parents' room at no extra charge, but others charge for them as extra adults; find out the cut-off age for discounts.

Hotels have private bathrooms, phones, and TVs, and don't offer meals unless we specify a meal plan in the review (i.e., breakfast, some meals, all meals, all-inclusive). We always list facilities but not whether you'll be charged an extra fee to use them.

For lodging price categories, consult the price chart at the beginning of the Where to Stay chapter.

APARTMENT AND HOUSE RENTALS

Apartments and time-share condos are common in Aruba. So if you're looking for more space for your family or group to spread out in (and especially if you want to have access to a kitchen to make some meals), this can be a very budget-friendly option. The money you save can be used for more dining and activities. Many time-share resorts are full-service, offering the same range of water sports and other activities as any other resort. And some regular resorts also have a time-share component.

HOTELS

Aruba is a major tourist destination and offers a variety of hotel types. Most hotels are in one of two stretches: the low-rise hotels in a stretch along Druif Beach and Eagle Beach, and the high-rise hotels on a stretch of Palm Beach. With a few exceptions, the hotels in the high-rise area tend to be larger and more expensive than their low-rise counterparts, but they usually offer a wider range of services.

ADDRESSES

"Informal" might best describe Aruban addresses. Sometimes the street designation is in English (as in J. E. Irausquin Boulevard), other times in Dutch (as in Wilhelminastraat); sometimes it's not specified whether something is a boulevard or a *straat* (street) at all. Street numbers follow street names, and postal codes aren't used. In rural areas you might have to ask a local for directions—and be prepared for such instructions as "Take a right at the market, then a left where you see the big divi-divi tree."

COMMUNICATIONS

INTERNET

Resortwide free Wi-Fi is not as common as you might think—many still charge daily rates for access in your room and other parts of the property—but many hotels and resorts do offer free Wi-Fi in their lobby for guests and a few desktop computers in their business centers. Many bars and dining spots and even stores now offer free Wi-Fi; just ask them for the password when you order something.

PHONES

To call Aruba direct from the United States, dial 011–297, followed by the seven-digit number in Aruba. International, direct, and operator-assisted calls from Aruba to all countries in the world are possible via hotel operators or from the Government Long Distance Telephone, Telegraph, and Radio Office (SETAR), in the post-office building in Oranjestad. When making calls on Aruba, simply dial the seven-digit number. AT&T customers can dial 800–8000 from special phones at the cruise dock and in the airport's arrival and departure halls and charge calls to their credit card. From other phones, dial 121 to contact the SETAR international operator to place a collect or AT&T calling-card call.

LOCAL CALLS

Dial the seven-digit number.

CALLING THE UNITED STATES

Dial 0, then 1, the area code, and the number.

CALLING CARDS

Aruba does not have a lot of pay phones anymore, and using them can be a challenge. You are better off with a prepaid SIM card. Aruba has both 3G and 4G cellular networks. Cards are available at the airport and at shops; both major communications providers, SETAR and Digicel, offer them.

MOBILE PHONES

Both SETAR and Digicel offer rental phones, but take note of the cost, as the rental charges and deposit may make purchasing a cheap phone a better choice, especially if you're staying more than a week. Most U.S.–based GSM and CDMA cell phones work on Aruba.

If you have a multiband phone (some countries use frequencies different from those used in the United States) and your service provider uses the world-standard

GSM network (as do T-Mobile, AT&T Mobility, and Verizon), you can probably use your phone abroad. Roaming fees can be steep. And overseas you normally pay the toll charges for incoming calls. It's almost always cheaper to send a text message than to make a call.

If you just want to make local calls, consider buying a new SIM card (note that your provider may have to unlock your phone for you to use a different SIM card) and a prepaid service plan in the destination. You'll then have a local number and can make local calls at local rates. If your trip is extensive, you could also simply buy a new cell phone in your destination, as the initial cost will be offset over time.

■TIP→ If you travel internationally frequently, save one of your old mobile phones or buy a cheap one on the Internet; ask your cell-phone company to unlock it for you, and take it with you as a travel phone, buying a new SIM card with pay-as-you-go service in each destination.

Contacts Aruba Cellular
☎ 297/563–1500 ⊕ www.aruba cellular.com. **Aruba Discount Cell** ☎ 297/732–8809 ⊕ www. arubadiscountcell.com. **Digicel** ☎ 297/522–2222 ⊕ www.digicel aruba.com. **SETAR.** Beyond cellular plans and cell rentals, you can also rent a portable Internet hot spot called Mi-Fi from this company during your stay, meaning you will have Internet wherever you go on the island. It's more affordable than roaming, and small and lightweight, too. ☎ 297/525–1000 ⊕ www.setar.aw.

▐ CUSTOMS AND DUTIES

You can bring up to 1 liter of spirits, 3 liters of beer, or 2.25 liters of wine per person, and up to 200 cigarettes or 50 cigars into Aruba. You don't need to declare the value of gifts or other items, although customs officials may inquire about large items or large quantities of goods and charge (at their discretion) an import tax of 7.5%–22% on items worth more than $230. Meat, birds, and illegal substances are forbidden. You may be asked to provide written verification that plants are free of diseases. If you're traveling with pets, bring a veterinarian's note attesting to their good health.

Aruba Information Aruba Customs Office ☎ 297/582–1800 ⊕ www.douane.aw.

U.S. Information U.S. Customs and Border Protection ⊕ www. cbp.gov.

▐ EATING OUT

Unless otherwise noted, the restaurants listed *in this guide* are open daily for lunch and dinner.

Aruba offers a startling variety of eating options thanks to the tourist trade, with choices ranging from upscale to simple roadside dining. The island is also a particularly family-friendly destination, so bringing the kids along is rarely a problem, and many restaurants offer children's menus.

ARUBAN CUISINE

Aruba shares many of its traditional foods with Bonaire and Curaçao. These dishes are a fusion of the various influences that have shaped the culture of the islands. Proximity to mainland South America means that many traditional snack and breakfast foods of Venezuelan origin, such as *empanadas* (fried cornmeal dumplings filled with ground meat), are widely found. The Dutch influence is evident in the fondness for cheese of all sorts, but especially Gouda. *Keshi yena,* ground meat or seafood with seasonings and placed in a hollowed-out cheese rind before baking, is a national dish.

If there's one thread that unites the cuisines of the Caribbean, it's cornmeal, and Arubans love nothing more than a side of *funchi* (like a thick polenta) or a *pan bati* (a fried cornmeal pancake) to make a traditional meal complete. Though Aruban cuisine isn't by nature spicy, it's almost always accompanied by a small bowl of spicy *pika* (a condiment of fiery hot peppers and onions in vinegar) or a bottle of hot sauce made from local peppers. An abundance of seafood means that seafood is the most popular protein on the island, and it's been said that if there were an Aruban national dish, it would be the catch of the day.

CELL PHONE TIPS

You can purchase a cheap cell phone at numerous outlets and simply "top up" (pay as you go). Incoming calls are free, so have your family call you to save on exorbitant island rates and huge roaming charges. Not all cell phones from home will work in Aruba (some do, but you never know which ones until you're actually on-island), even if the phone company tells you it does.

PAYING

We assume that restaurants and hotels accept credit cards. If they don't, we'll note it in the review.

For guidelines on tipping see Tipping, below.

RESERVATIONS AND DRESS

We mention reservations only when they're essential (there's no other way you'll ever get a table) or when they're not accepted. We mention dress only when men are required to wear a jacket or a jacket and tie.

WINES, BEER, AND SPIRITS

Arubans have a great love for wine, so even small supermarkets have a fairly good selection of European and South American wines at prices that are reasonable by Caribbean standards. The beer of choice in Aruba is the island-brewed Balashi and the newer Balashi Chill often served with a wedge of lime, though many also favor the deliciously crisp Amstel Bright, which is brewed on nearby Curaçao. Local spirits also include *ponce crema,* a wickedly potent eggnog type of liqueur.

▮ ELECTRICITY

Aruba runs on a 110-volt cycle, the same as in the United States; outlets are usually the two-prong variety. Total blackouts are rare, and most large hotels have back-up generators.

▮ EMERGENCIES

The number to call in case of emergency (911) is the same as in the United States.

▮ HEALTH

As a rule, water is pure and food is wholesome in hotels and local restaurants throughout Aruba, but be cautious when buying food from street vendors. And just as you would at home, wash or peel all fruits and vegetables before eating them. Traveler's diarrhea, caused by consuming contaminated water, unpasteurized milk and milk products, and unrefrigerated food, isn't a big problem—unless it happens to you. So watch what you eat, especially at outdoor buffets in the hot sun. Make sure cooked food is hot and cold food has been properly refrigerated.

The major health risk is sunburn or sunstroke. A long-sleeve shirt, a hat, and long pants or a beach wrap are essential on a boat, for midday at the beach, and whenever you go out sightseeing. Use sunscreen with an SPF of at least 15—especially if you're fair-skinned—and apply it liberally to your nose, ears, and other sensitive and exposed areas. Make sure the sunscreen is waterproof if you're engaging in water sports. Always limit your sun time for the first few days, and drink plenty of liquids. Limit intake of caffeine and alcohol, which hasten dehydration.

Mosquitoes and flies can be bothersome, so pack strong repellent (the ones that contain DEET or Picaridin are the most effective). The strong trade winds are a relief in the subtropical climate, but don't hang your bathing suit on a balcony—it'll probably blow away. Help Arubans conserve water and energy: turn off air-conditioning when you leave your room, and don't let water run unattended.

Don't fly within 24 hours of scuba diving. In an emergency, Air Ambulance, run by Richard Rupert, will fly you to Curaçao at a low altitude if you need to get to a decompression chamber.

OVER-THE-COUNTER REMEDIES

There are a number of pharmacies and stores selling simple medications throughout the island (including at most hotels), and virtually anything obtainable in North America is available in Aruba.

SHOTS AND MEDICATIONS

No special vaccinations are required to visit Aruba.

Health Warnings Centers for Disease Control & Prevention (*CDC*). ☎ *877/394–8747 for international travelers' health line* ⊕ *www.cdc. gov/travel.* **World Health Organization** (*WHO*). ⊕ *www.who.int.*

HOURS OF OPERATION

Most of Aruba's services, like banks, are basically open the same hours you'd expect in North America, though some spots will close on Sunday and on national holidays. Most modern conveniences are available seven days a week.

HOLIDAYS

Aruba's official holidays are New Year's Day, Good Friday, Easter Sunday, and Christmas, as well as Betico Croes Day (January 25), National Anthem and Flag Day (March 18), King's Day (April 30), Labor Day (May 1), and Ascension Day (May 5 in 2016).

MAIL

From Aruba to the United States or Canada a letter costs Afl2.20 (about $1.25) and a postcard costs Afl1.30 (75¢). Expect it to take one to two weeks. When addressing letters to Aruba, don't worry about the lack of formal addresses or postal codes; the island's postal service knows where to go.

If you need to send a package in a hurry, there are a few options. The Federal Express office across from the airport offers overnight service to the United States if you get your package in before 3 pm. Another big courier service is UPS, and several smaller local courier services, most of them open weekdays 9–5, also provide international deliveries. Check the local phone book for details.

SHIPPING PACKAGES

Federal Express service is available in downtown Oranjestad.

Contacts FedEx ⊠ *Browninvest Financial Center, Wayaca 31-A, Oranjestad* ☎ *297/592–9039* ⊕ *www. fedex.com/aw*. **UPS** ⊠ *L. G. Smith Blvd. 128, Oranjestad* ☎ *297/588– 0640* ⊕ *www.ups.com/content/ aw/en/contact/index.html?WT. svl=Footer.*

MONEY

Arubans happily accept U.S. dollars virtually everywhere. That said, there's no real need to exchange money, except for necessary pocket change (for soda machines or pay phones). The official currency is the Aruban florin (Afl), also called the guilder, which is made up of 100 cents. Silver coins come in denominations of 1, 2½, 5, 10, 25, and 50 (the square one) cents. Paper currency comes in denominations of 5, 10, 25, 50, and 100 florins.

Prices quoted *throughout this book* are in U.S. dollars unless otherwise noted and are given for adults. Substantially reduced fees are almost always available for children, students, and senior citizens.

ATMS AND BANKS

If you need fast cash, you'll find ATMs that accept international cards (and dispense cash in both U.S. and local currency) at banks in Oranjestad, at major malls, and along roads leading to the hotel strip.

Banks Caribbean Mercantile Bank ⊠ *Palm Beach 4B, Noord* ☎ *297/586–0200* ⊕ *www.cmbnv. com.* **Aruba RBC Bank** ⊠ *Caya G. F. Betico Croes 89, Oranjestad* ☎ *297/588–0101* ⊕ *aw.rbcnetbank. com.*

CREDIT CARDS

It's a good idea to inform your credit-card company before you travel, especially if you're going abroad and don't travel internationally very often. Otherwise, the credit-card company might put a hold on your card owing to unusual activity—not a good thing halfway through your trip. Record all your credit-card numbers—as well as the phone numbers to call if your cards are lost or stolen—in a safe place, so you're prepared should something go wrong. Both MasterCard and Visa have general numbers you can call (collect if you're abroad) if your card is lost, but you're better off calling the number of your issuing bank, since MasterCard and Visa usually just transfer you to your bank; your bank's number is usually printed on your card.

If you plan to use your credit card for cash advances, you'll need to apply for a PIN at least two weeks before your trip. Although it's usually cheaper (and safer) to use a credit card abroad for large purchases (so you can cancel payments or be reimbursed if there's a problem), note that some credit-card companies *and* the banks that issue them add substantial percentages to all foreign transactions, whether they're in a foreign currency or not. Check on these fees before leaving home, so there won't be any surprises when you get the bill.

Reporting Lost Cards American Express ☎ 800/528–4800 in the U.S., 336/393–1111 collect from abroad ⊕ www.americanexpress. com. **MasterCard** ☎ 800/627–8372 in the U.S., 636/722–7111 collect from abroad ⊕ www.mastercard.com. **Visa** ☎ 800/847–2911 in the U.S., 800–1518 aruba ⊕ www.visa.com.

CURRENCY EXCHANGE

At this writing, exchange rates were Afl1.56 to the U.S. dollar and Afl1.68 to the Canadian dollar. The Dutch Antillean florin—used on Bonaire and Curaçao—isn't accepted here. Since U.S. dollars are universally accepted, few people exchange money.

Currency Conversion Google ⊕ www.google.com. **Oanda.com** ⊕ www.oanda.com. **XE.com** ⊕ www. xe.com.

▌ PACKING

Dress on Aruba is generally casual. Bring loose-fitting clothing made of natural fabrics to see you through days of heat and humidity. Pack a beach cover-up, both to protect yourself from the sun and to provide something to wear to and from your hotel room. Bathing suits and immodest attire are frowned upon away from the beach. A sun hat is advisable, but you don't have to pack one—inexpensive straw hats are available everywhere. For shopping and sightseeing, bring walking shorts, jeans, T-shirts, long-sleeve cotton shirts, slacks, and sundresses. Nighttime dress can range from very informal to casually elegant, depending on the establishment. A tie is practically never required, but a jacket may be appropriate in fancy restaurants. You may need a light sweater or jacket for evening.

PASSPORTS AND VISAS

A valid passport is required to enter or reenter the United States from Aruba.

RESTROOMS

Outside Oranjestad, public restrooms can be found in dining and small restaurants that dot the countryside.

SAFETY

Arubans are very friendly, so you needn't be afraid to stop and ask anyone for directions. It's a relatively safe island, but common-sense rules still apply. Lock your rental car when you leave it, and leave valuables in your hotel safe. Don't leave bags unattended in the airport, on the beach, or on tour vehicles.

TIP→ Distribute your cash, credit cards, IDs, and other valuables between a deep front pocket, an inside jacket or vest pocket, and a hidden money pouch.

Contact Transportation Security Administration (*TSA*). ⊕ *www.tsa. gov.*

TAXES

The airport departure tax is $37 for flights to the United States and $33.50 to other destinations, but the fee is usually included in your ticket price. Children under two don't pay departure tax. For purchases you'll pay a 3% BBO tax (a turnover tax on each level of sale for all goods and services) in all but the duty-free shops.

TIME

Aruba is in the Atlantic standard time zone, which is one hour later than eastern standard time or four hours earlier than Greenwich mean time. During daylight saving time, April–October, Atlantic standard is the same time as eastern daylight time.

Time Zones Timeanddate.com ⊕ *www.timeanddate.com/worldclock.*

TIPPING

Restaurants generally include a 10%–15% service charge on the bill; when in doubt, ask. If service isn't included, a 15% tip is standard; if it's included, it's still customary to add something extra, usually small change, at your discretion. Taxi drivers expect a 10%–15% tip, but it isn't mandatory. Porters and bellhops should receive about $2 per bag; chambermaids about $2 per day, but check to see if their tips are included in your bill so you don't overpay.

TOURS

You can see the main sights in one day, but set aside two days to really meander. Guided tours are your best option if you have only a short time.

TOUR OPERATORS

There are many first-rate tour operators on Aruba, and the adventures range from wild and crazy jeep safaris in the outback to Segway tours along the coast to sea and sand discovery and animal attractions. A good way to get your bearings is to take a bus tour around the island's main highlights—it's a small island so it will not take more than half a day—with a well-established company like De Palm Tours.

SPECIAL-INTEREST TOURS

BOATING

If you try a cruise around the island, know that the choppy waters are stirred up by trade winds and that catamarans are much smoother than single-hulled boats. Sucking on a peppermint or lemon candy may help a queasy stomach; avoid boating with an empty or overly full stomach. Snorkeling and sunset party cruises are the norm, but some also include dinner or have dinner on shore after your voyage. Most seaborne tours depart from Palm Beach at either Pelican Pier or De Palm Pier.

Contacts Red Sail Sports ⊠ *Renaissance Mall, L. G. Smith Blvd. 82, Oranjestad* ☎ *297/586–1603, 877/733–7245 in the U.S.* ⊕ *www.aruba-redsail.com.*

SUBMARINE TOURS

You can explore an underwater reef teeming with marine life without getting wet. Atlantis Submarines (operated by De Palm Tours) operates a 65-foot air-conditioned sub that takes 48 passengers 95–130 feet below the surface along Barcadera Reef. The two-hour trip (including boat transfer to the submarine platform and 50-minute plunge) celebrated its 25th year of operation in 2015 and has multiple awards for best tour and one for green operations. Make reservations one day in advance. Another option is the *Seaworld Explorer,*

a semisubmersible also operated by Atlantis Submarines that allows you to view Aruba's marine habitat from six feet below the surface.

Contacts Atlantis Submarines ⊠ *Renaissance Marina* ☎ *297/582–4400* ⊕ *www.depalmtours.com/atlantis-submarines-expedition.*

▐ TRIP INSURANCE

Comprehensive travel policies typically cover trip cancellation and interruption, letting you cancel or cut your trip short because of a personal emergency, illness, or, in some cases, acts of terrorism in your destination. Such policies also cover evacuation and medical care. Some also cover you for trip delays because of bad weather or mechanical problems as well as for lost or delayed baggage. Another type of coverage to look for is financial default—that is, when your trip is disrupted because a tour operator, airline, or cruise line goes out of business. Generally you must buy this when you book your trip or shortly thereafter, and it's available to you only if your operator isn't on a list of excluded companies.

At the very least, consider buying medical-only coverage. Neither Medicare nor some private insurers cover medical expenses anywhere outside the United States (including time aboard a cruise ship, even if it leaves from a U.S. port). Medical-only policies typically reimburse you for medical care (excluding care related to preexisting conditions) and hospitalization abroad, and provide for evacuation. You still have to pay the bills and await reimbursement from the insurer, though.

Another option is to sign up with a medical-evacuation assistance company. A membership in one of these companies gets you doctor referrals, emergency evacuation or repatriation, 24-hour hotlines for medical consultation, and other assistance. International SOS and AirMed International provide evacuation services and medical referrals. MedjetAssist offers medical evacuation.

Expect comprehensive travel insurance policies to cost about 4%–8% of the total price of your trip (it's more like 8%–12% if you're over age 70). A medical-only policy may or may not be cheaper than a comprehensive policy. Always read the fine print of your policy to make sure that you're covered for the risks that are of most concern to you. Compare several policies to make sure you're getting the best price and range of coverage available.

Comprehensive Travel Insurers
AIG Travel Guard ☎ 800/826–4919 ⊕ www.travelguard.com. **CSA Travel Protection** ☎ 877/243–4135 in the U.S. ⊕ www.csatravelprotection.com. **HTH Worldwide** ☎ 888/243–2358 ⊕ www.hthworldwide.com. **Travel Insured International** ☎ 800/243–3174 ⊕ www.travelinsured.com. **Travelex Insurance** ☎ 888/228–9792 ⊕ www.travelex-insurance.com.

Insurance Comparison Sites **Insure My Trip.com** ☎ 800/551–1337 ⊕ www.insuremytrip.com. **Square Mouth.com** ☎ 800/240–0369, 727/490–5803 ⊕ www.square mouth.com.

Medical Assistance Companies
AirMed International Medical Group ☎ 800/356–2161 ⊕ www.airmed.com. **International SOS** ☎ 800/527–7278 ⊕ www.internationalsos.com. **MedjetAssist** ⊕ www.medjetassist.com.

Medical-Only Insurers **International Medical Group** ☎ 800/628–4664 ⊕ www.imglobal.com. **Wallach & Company** ☎ 800/237–6615, 540/687–3166 ⊕ www.wallach.com.

▮ VISITOR INFORMATION

Before leaving home, research online about all Aruba has to offer at their tourism authority's website ⊕ *www.aruba.com*. They also have a handy app you can download to your smartphone.

Aruba Information Aruba Tourism Authority ✉ L. G. Smith Blvd. 172, Eagle Beach ☎ 800/862–7822 in the U.S./abroad, 297/582–3777 in Aruba ⊕ www.aruba.com.

▮ WEDDINGS

People over the age of 18 can marry as long as they submit the appropriate documents 14 days in advance. Couples are required to submit birth certificates with raised seals, through the mail or in person, to Aruba's Office of the Civil Registry. They also need an apostil—a document proving they're free to marry—from their country of residence. Same-sex ceremonies are also available on Aruba, though they're not legally binding.

With so many beautiful spots to choose from, weddings on Aruba are guaranteed to be romantic.

Fodor's Choice ★ **Aruba Fairy Tales Weddings.** Founder Indira Maduro has been planning weddings on Aruba for more than a decade, helping visitors tie the knot or renew their vows on the island's most beautiful beaches in high style. Recently her company has branched out to also specialize in LGBT weddings under the name G+L Weddings, provided as a separate service. They can plan pre- and post-wedding activities on the island for your group as well. ☎ 297/993–0045 ⊕ *www.aruba fairytales.com.*

Aruba Weddings for You. The official wedding-planning service of the Divi family of resorts on Aruba, this is a full-service operation that can take care of everything from scouting the location to arranging a trash-the-dress photo shoot. Specializing in romantic beach weddings, they can also help with all paperwork and planning with a civil-ceremony package. ☎ 297/525–5293 ⊕ *www.aruba weddingsforyou.com.*

INDEX

PHOTO CREDITS

Front cover: DanitaDelimont / AWL Images Ltd [Description: Oranjestad, Aruba]. Spine: Zazen | Dreamstime.com. 1, Holger W./Shutterstock. 2, Corey Weiner /Red Square, Inc. 3, (top), Göran Ingman / Flickr, [CC BY-542.0] 3 (bottom), Red Square, Inc. 4 (top), Aruba Tourism Authority. 4 (bottom), Courtesy of Kukoo Kunuku. 5 (top), Rebecca Genin/Aruba Tourism. 5 (bottom) and 6 (top), Aruba Tourism Authority. 6 (bottom), Passions on the Beach. 7, Vilainecrevette/Shutterstock. 8 (top), Jack Jackson / age fotostock. 8 (bottom), Aruba Tourism Authority. 10, Corey Weiner/redsquarephoto.com/Marriott. Chapter 1: Experience Aruba: 12-13, Aruba Tourism Authority. 14 and 15 (left), Rebecca Genin/Aruba Tourism. 15 (right), jeff gynane/Shutterstock. 18 and 19, Aruba Tourism Authority. 20, Rebecca Genin/Aruba Tourism. 22, David P. Smith/Shutterstock. Chapter 2: Exploring: 23, Aruba Tourism Authority. 26-27, Donaldford | Dreamstime.com. 34, Sarah Bossert/iStockphoto. 36-37, Kjorgen | Dreamstime. com. 38, Aruba Tourism Authority. 42-43, Paul D'Innocenzo. Chapter 3: Beaches: 45, Zazen | Dreamstime.com. 47, Kjersti Joergensen/Shutterstock. 48-49, Marriott. Chapter 4: Where to Eat: 53, Madame Janette's. 58, Kenneth Theysen | Timeless-Pixx. 68, Madame Janette's. Chapter 5: Where to Stay: 77, Corey Weiner/redsquarephoto.com/Marriott. 81, Marriott. 84, Bucuti Beach Resort. 86-87 Famke Backx/iStockphoto. 88, Amsterdam Manor Beach Resort Aruba. 90, Corey Weiner/redsquarephoto.com/Marriott. Chapter 6: Nightlife and the Performing Arts: 93, Bas Rabeling/Shutterstock. 96, Aruba Tourism Authority. 100-101, Stuart Pearce / age fotostock. Chapter 7: Casinos: 107, Aruba Tourism Authority. 109, The Ritz Carlton, Aruba. 113, Corey Weiner/redsquarephoto. com/Marriott. 117, Aruba Marriott Stellaris Casino & Resort. Chapter 8: Sports and the Outdoors: 123, Aruba Tourism Authority. 125, 126, and 129, Corey Weiner/redsquarephoto.com/Marriott. 130, Marriott. 136-137, Svitlana Prada/ iStockphoto. 138, Rebecca Genin/Aruba Tourism. 141, Paul D'Innocenzo. Chapter 9: Shopping: 143, Starwood Hotels & Resorts. 149, madmack66/Flickr. 154, Aruba Tourism Authority.

NOTES

NOTES

NOTES

NOTES

NOTES

NOTES

NOTES

NOTES

NOTES

NOTES

NOTES

Fodor's InFocus ARUBA

Publisher: Amanda D'Acierno, *Senior Vice President*

Editorial: Arabella Bowen, *Editor in Chief*; Linda Cabasin, *Editorial Director*

Design: Tina Malaney, *Associate Art Director*; Chie Ushio, *Senior Designer*

Photography: Jennifer Arnow, *Senior Photo Editor*; Mary Robnett, *Photo Researcher*

Production: Linda Schmidt, *Managing Editor*; Evangelos Vasilakis, *Associate Managing Editor*; Angela L. McLean, *Senior Production Manager*

Maps: Rebecca Baer, *Senior Map Editor*; David Lindroth, Ed Jacobus, William Wu, with additional cartography provided by Henry Columb, Mark Stroud, and Ali Baird, Moon Street Cartography, *Cartographers*

Sales: Jacqueline Lebow, *Sales Director*

Marketing & Publicity: Heather Dalton, *Marketing Director*; Katherine Punia, *Publicity Director*

Business & Operations: Susan Livingston, *Vice President, Strategic Business Planning*; Sue Daulton, *Vice President, Operations*

Fodors.com: Megan Bell, *Executive Director, Revenue & Business Development*; Yasmin Marinaro, *Senior Director, Marketing & Partnerships*

Copyright © 2016 by Fodor's Travel, a division of Penguin Random House LLC

Writer: Susan Campbell
Series editor: Douglas Stallings
Editor: Perrie Hartz
Production Editor: Carrie Parker

5th Edition

ISBN 978-1-101-87957-3

ISSN 1939-988X

SPECIAL SALES

This book is available at special discounts for bulk purchases for sales promotions or premiums. For more information, e-mail specialmarkets@penguinrandomhouse.com.

PRINTED IN THE UNITED STATES OF AMERICA

10 9 8 7 6 5 4 3 2 1

ABOUT OUR WRITER

 Based in Montreal, Canada, Susan Campbell is an award-winning travel writer. She has been an expert on the Dutch Caribbean for over 20 years and is the major contributor to the on-island guides of Aruba, Bonaire, Curacao and St. Maarten for Nights Publications. Susan visits Aruba several times a year and has extensive knowledge of the island and its culture, history, and attractions, which she shares via multiple online and print outlets throughout North America.